CONTENTS

PREFACE

———— * ————

On grounds both of aesthetics and intelligibility, few would follow Cosimo de' Medici in choosing the *Philebus* as his death-bed literature, even if the translator and reader were Marsilio Ficino. The style of the dialogue is occasionally turgid, the meaning often far from clear. Both sorts of obscurity are the province of the translator. My policy as regards the stylistic density has been to try and make the dialogue readable; but at some points I have found it impossible not to reproduce the somewhat stilted nature of the Greek, especially where this occurs in the first place for the sake of philosophical complete-ness. Obscurity of meaning, on the other hand, is usually im-possible to remove by fair translation. Yet the translator has to understand his text in order to provide a meaningful transla-tion. Consequently, as has often been remarked, any transla-tion of a complex work is bound to reflect partisan views of certain passages: *traduttore-traditore*. I have tried to explain and to some extent justify my understanding of the general pur-pose of the dialogue in the Introduction, though this, even in combination with the footnotes which deal with minor exege-tical points that might need elucidation while the dialogue is being read, still falls far short of being a complete commentary on the dialogue. The *Philebus*, more than many Platonic dialogues, stands in need of an Introduction. Although it is unique in being Plato's most deliberate attempt to describe the 'good life', and therefore occupies an important place in his writings, the interpretation of several crucial passages is far from certain.

The purpose of the Introduction, then, is to guide the reader through the course of each of the main stages of the dialogue, but also to point out occasionally certain weaknesses in the arguments. Readers who are not already philosophers or historians of philosophy may find this aspect excessively critical and wonder why they should bother to read the dialogue, if it is flawed. My response is to emphasize from the start that though Plato's arguments are often unsatisfactory (and this applies to the majority of the dialogues), this does not affect the correctness, or at least interest, of his particular conclusions and his general strategy. Indeed, it is arguable that Plato was always more concerned about conclusions than the arguments used to reach them. There is, I believe, much in the *Philebus* to interest the general reader, whether he turns to it looking for a way of life, or out of intellectual curiosity.

Many friends and colleagues have helped me on one or more points during the preparation of this book. I owe debts of gratitude in particular to Mrs Betty Radice, for advice and encouragement; to Professor Ian Kidd, for a number of improvements; especially to Professor Tony Woodman and Dr Malcolm Schofield for painstaking work on the translation and Introduction respectively; and last, but not least, to my wife, Briji, who patiently went through every stage of the translation and endures, with equal fortitude, my frequent preoccupation.

INTRODUCTION

———— * ————

THE CHARACTERS OF THE DIALOGUE

Socrates will need little introduction. He was born in 469 BC and died in 399, condemned to death by his fellow Athenians on the charges of irreligion and immoral teaching. Since he never committed himself to writing, we can know very little for certain of his thought. The only contemporary witness is the comic playwright, Aristophanes, who used Socrates in the *Clouds* as a figurehead for intellectuals of all kinds: he cannot, then, be treated as evidence for what Socrates himself was concerned with. We have to rely mainly on the writings of Plato and Xenophon, both self-confessed admirers of Socrates, part of whose purpose in writing was to defend their mentor posthumously. In the earliest dialogues he wrote, Plato gives us a lively picture of a keen and ironic mind at work. But in the *Philebus* we are far from the Socrates of those dialogues. There Socrates dissembles, lays no claim to knowledge, and is consequently concerned merely to question his interlocutor, invariably to find faults in what that unfortunate person may think. In the *Philebus*, however, Protarchus has little to say for himself, while Socrates continually puts forward positive doctrine. The mode of questioning is still used, but not in conjunction with a portrayal of an apparently ignorant Socrates. It may fairly be assumed that part, at any rate, of Plato's purpose in the earliest dialogues was simply to present his contemporaries with a picture of Socrates such that they must wonder why they and their fathers ever condemned him to death. But in the *Philebus* Plato is hardly concerned with dramatic portrayal: his main concern is the philosophical problem of the dialogue –

how should we conduct ourselves, or, as the Greeks would put it, what is the good life? – and Socrates is merely the mouthpiece for Plato's ideas on this topic.

The introduction and asides of other dialogues often make the dramatic setting of the conversation come alive (e.g. the gymnasium, so-and-so's house): not so the *Philebus*. Nor are we given enough information to make a guess about the dramatic date of the dialogue (as, most obviously, 'the day of Socrates' death in 399' for the *Phaedo*). As with other aspects of Plato's art as a writer, there are only traces of such embellishments: we do hear from time to time that there are several persons present at the conversation. The only two we meet, however, are Protarchus and Philebus.

Protarchus is a young man, son of Callias (19b), pupil of Gorgias, the famous teacher of rhetoric and sophistic philosopher (58a ff.). I see no reason to doubt that he is the Protarchus mentioned by Aristotle at *Physics* 197b as the author of an apparently sophistic argument.

Philebus is a different kettle of fish. The arguments for and against his being an historical person are equally strong. On the one hand, if both Socrates and Protarchus are real people, it would be odd for Philebus not to be too. The fact that his name could be taken to be rather appropriate for his hedonism (Mr Loveboy, as one commentator has put it) is neither here nor there: a better translation might be Youth-friend, and this is certainly no more odd than many of the Greek names we know of. A later Greek writer, Alciphron, uses the name in one of his fictional Epistles (III.14), but he could have lifted it from our dialogue. But the portrayal of Philebus is just vivid enough to make it possible that Plato has a real person in mind: he is sullenly stubborn (12a–b), a bad loser (11c) and, of course, a hedonist. He might be an older man (16b), of a similar age, then, to Socrates.

He plays very little part in the dialogue: why, then, is it named after him? Because the doctrine of pleasure which occupies a major part of the dialogue is built up against the background of the sort of hedonism that Philebus espoused.

Protarchus is only a stand-in for Philebus, the dramatic idea being that because pleasure is irrational, a hedonist is unimpressed by Socratic reasoning, and an amenable interlocutor must be found.

It is precisely the fact that Philebus is the silent figurehead of hedonism that lends credibility to the view that he is a product of Plato's imagination. One of the remarkable features of the *Philebus* is the wealth of references in it to other thinkers and schools of thought. Plato draws on Pythagoreanism (16c ff.), argues against an extension of Heracliteanism (42e ff.), against Gorgias (58a–e) and perhaps Protagoras (57d). The background of 28–31 is Presocratic (see p. 80 n.2), and several other similar references can be detected. Two unidentifiable thinkers or schools of thought, probably contemporaries of Plato's, are characterized as the 'well-bred' philosophers (44a ff., perhaps Speusippus, Plato's nephew and fellow Academician) and the 'subtle' thinkers (53c ff.). Perhaps, then, we should infer that Philebus is a fictional representative of the position of some contemporary hedonist: Eudoxus of Cnidus is the best bet. However we learn from Aristotle, *Nicomachean Ethics* 1172b, that despite adopting a hedonist position, which was certainly similar in many respects to Philebus', Eudoxus himself, unlike Philebus, was very self-controlled. If Philebus is a fictional character, it seems safest to suppose that he stands for hedonism in general, rather than Eudoxus in particular. Personally, however, I incline to think that Philebus was an historical person.

THE DATE OF THE COMPOSITION OF THE DIALOGUE

The vast majority of scholars believe that the *Philebus* was of the last dialogues Plato ever wrote, i.e. that it was written in the late 350s. While I myself doubt this (see my article on the subject in *Phronesis* 1980, pp. 270–305), I do not intend to try and persuade the readers of this volume of my views the dialogue can well be read without immediate reference to other Platonic dialogues.

THE CONTEMPORARY BACKGROUND

The Athens of the time of Socrates (469–399) and of Plato (427–347) must have been an intellectually exciting place to live. The city, having risen to a zenith of political and cultural power, succeeded in attracting many of the great names in Greek philosophy as visitors or residents. This tradition continued, with Plato rather than Athens as the magnet, even after the downfall of the city in the Peloponnesian War (431–404). In 386, or thereabouts, Plato purchased some land and a building in an area sacred to the local hero Academos, and established an institution for education and research which became known as the Academy. Little is known of the studies that were pursued in the Academy beyond the fact that it concentrated on science and philosophy, but sufficient prestige attached to association with it for several of its members to be invited to codify the laws of various Greek cities. Moreover many gifted thinkers were drawn to the Academy, the most famous of them being Aristotle. One thing we can be sure of is that the Academy was no mere vehicle for the promulgation of Platonism: its members were free to agree or disagree with Plato.

The intellectual climate in Athens at the end of the fifth and beginning of the fourth centuries, then, was one in which many different theories about many different matters were being proposed. The interest of the period, however, lies not just in the variety of thought, but in the common ground these thinkers share. The sixth and early fifth centuries had been dominated by several more or less dogmatic theories about the origin and physical nature of the universe, its inhabitants and features. Not that this trend died out in the time of Socrates and Plato, but their period was also involved in formulation of questions of a different kind. Human beings act in certain ways: why? What leads a man to prefer one course of action to another? For the first time philosophical answers to this question were being sought. A great debate, for instance, among the intellectuals of the fifth century in particular was whether man was conditioned by his natural or his social environment, and by which was it right for him to be conditioned. Another direction the inquiry took – and this is of special relevance to the *Philebus* – was to formulate the ideals men have in view for themselves. That is, what does a man consider to be the good? Is it sensual pleasure, or honour, or a life devoted to the intellect? And *should* a man be motivated by a desire to maximize his pleasure or whatever?

An important feature of this debate, which must have contributed to the excitement of the times, is that it is no mere academic investigation, but an inquiry into what actually motivated people. These thinkers were *beginning* ethical discussion: their theories were not just evolved to combat another thinker's theory, or some part of it, but as a positive attempt to explain human motivation. So the terms of Plato's and his contemporaries' studies were, what is the good *life*? Thus, on the whole (but see p. 43), the *Philebus* is a directly ethical, rather than meta-ethical, work: as Aristotle put it in his *Nicomachean Ethics*, 'we are studying not to know what goodness is, but how to become good men' (1103b 27–9).

As ethical debate progressed, the trichotomy of goods into pleasure, honour and knowledge soon became the accepted terms of the discussion, corresponding to bodily, external and internal goods. The Pythagoreans may have originated this trichotomy. Heraclides of Pontus (fragment 88) preserves an apocryphal story about Pythagoras, that he took the people who came to Olympia for the games to epitomize mankind in general: some came to do profitable business, some to compete for the prizes and some to observe and understand.

Pleasure is a natural candidate in the debate: 'There is implanted in the human mind a perception of pain and pleasure as the chief spring and moving principle of all its actions' (David Hume, 1711–76, *A Treatise of Human Nature*, I.3.10); 'Nature has placed mankind under the governance of two sovereign masters, pain and pleasure' (Jeremy Bentham, 1748–1832, *Principles of Morals and Legislation*, I.1). The point was not overlooked by Plato: 'Human nature involves, above all, pleasures, pains and desires, and no mortal animal can help being . . . in total dependence on these powerful influences' (*Laws* 732e).

The inclusion of honour in the list is just as well-grounded. Men are ambitious and they seek esteem in the eyes of others. For the Greeks in particular honour was as natural a candidate as pleasure. Homer, the eighth-century epic poet, adumbrated a value-system in which his heroes were concerned above all to avoid losing face among their peers and to gain honour. Although this value-system was geared to the archaic world, in which individuals were all-important, Homer was still a basis of Greek moral education in Plato's time.

Both pleasure and honour are worldly aims, but many will feel that the good life is not to be gained so cheaply. Should not such a life be more austere and other-worldly? Certainly there were those who felt this in ancient Greece, and so the life of pursuit of knowledge was proposed as the third ideal. This was not thought to be unnatural as distinct from the other two ideals: Aristotle was not alone in thinking that 'all men have an instinctive desire for knowledge' (*Metaphysics* 980a 21). But the philosophers understood knowledge in a special way, and this was a direct challenge to the view of Plato's contemporaries, which was that education was a fine thing as long as it was not indulged in to excess. Excess, on this view, lay in continuing with intellectual matters beyond one's childhood education, and perhaps a bit of dabbling into philosophy as a young man (cf. Plato, *Gorgias* 484c–d). This was enough to enable a gentleman to hold his own at symposia and to help him if he needed to compose an impressive speech. Certainly philosophy was not commonly held to be something to devote one's life to.

Some might be surprised that the Greeks had no ideal of the religious life. But it would be anachronistic to expect such an ideal. Greek personal religion, it must always be remembered, was non-dogmatic. As in our times, religion required the performance or non-performance of certain actions, and presumably it also required a certain emotional state, but it did not require affirmation of a body of doctrine. Very few disputes can have arisen about whether one was, or was not, religious, though it was possible to conform more or less with *state* religion. In other respects the modern ideal of the religious life is covered by the Greek ideal of the intellectual life. For instance, Plato argues in the *Phaedo* that the true philosopher, like a monk, is detached from the distractions of the body; and what theorizing there was about the nature of the gods and their relation to man was the province of the philosopher: hence philosophers were sometimes thought to be irreligious (Socrates was put on trial for this) and, much later, the early Christian theorists were concerned above all to combat the Greek philosophers, who, they realized, were their rivals in religious matters.

Aristotle dismisses hedonism as the view of the vulgar masses, while attributing the goal of honour to the more refined members of society (*Nicomachean Ethics* 1095b 16ff.): this again reminds us that even Aristotle feels he is trying to explain the actions that the members of his society actually performed, rather than theories that other thinkers had put forward. This approach contains a methodological danger: if I see someone pursuing pleasure all the time, is it right to infer that he is a hedonist, rather than someone whose goal is knowledge, but who fails to achieve his goal? But since these theorists were trying to formulate for the first time what motivates people, a working hypothesis had to be 'by their fruits you can judge them'. Philosophers before Plato and contemporary with him had found these three ideals in their fellows, and it is in this context that we should see the *Philebus*.

THE CONTRIBUTION OF THE PHILEBUS

The course of the dialogue is as follows. A preliminary discussion about pleasure and knowledge (11a–14a) throws up a methodological issue which is discussed but finally abandoned (14b–20b). The claims of both pleasure and knowledge to constitute the human good are abandoned in favour of some combination of them both (20b–23b). The relation of pleasure and knowledge to factors prevalent in the universe at large is discussed (23b–31b), before each of them is submitted to a thorough analysis (31b–55c, 55c–59d). The final topics are the nature of the good life and the relative importance of pleasure and knowledge within it (59d–67d).

It will be convenient to begin by considering the ethical doctrines of the dialogue before turning to the methodological and metaphysical passages (14b–20b, 23b–31b). These latter passages are not in fact employed in Plato's treatment of the central ethical questions of the dialogue. This is not to say that they are uninteresting: in fact many readers of a more metaphysical bent find them the most interesting parts of the dialogue.

In the terms of the ethical debate outlined in the previous pages, it is immediately noticeable that Plato devotes considerable time to discussing pleasure (31b–55c) and knowledge (55c–59d), but none to honour. There are two main reasons for this. In the first place a simple dichotomy is in conformity with both popular and more theoretical views on human nature. It was popularly held that man's *psyche* (the word is notoriously difficult to translate – the traditional translation, 'soul', has been adopted in this work) consisted of a rational and an irrational element: Plato takes it that the rational side of man is that which aims for knowledge, the irrational for pleasure. The more theoretical view of human nature, which is parallel to the popular view, is that man's nature partakes of both divinity and bestiality, the divine part being the intellect, the bestial part man's irrational and sensual side.

The second reason for the exclusion of honour is that though honour has a secure place in the Pythagorean trichotomy (and see also Plato, *Republic* 581c), it seems to have been held by the philosophers to be something of a maverick. Aristotle says (*Nicomachean Ethics* 1095b 23 ff.) that, if pressed, ambitious men would have to admit that their pursuit of honour was subordinate to a pursuit of goodness: so, whatever the good is, it

INTRODUCTION

is not the same as honour. He also makes the more obvious
point that honour is transient and therefore 'too superficial' to
be the *summum bonum*. Honour is certainly of less interest to the
philosopher: pleasure and knowledge and the pursuit of them
tell us something about the nature of the pursuant, but honour
tells us more about the nature of those conferring it than those
receiving it. These must be the sorts of reasons why Plato and
his philosophical contemporaries were prepared to discuss
pleasure and knowledge, and to advocate one or the other of
them as the goal of life, but ignored honour.

Plato, then, is concerned in the *Philebus* to weigh the merits
of pleasure and knowledge (11b–c). The first point to notice
about his discussion is that he is quick to prove that pleasure
cannot be altogether excluded from the good life (20b–22d),
otherwise the good life would not satisfy the criteria of perfection, sufficiency and desirability (20c–d); thus he avoids the
trap of thinking that pleasure and knowledge are mutually ex-
clusive ends. It might seem that this is a very easy trap to
avoid, but the hedonist position canvassed by Philebus (see
60a and p. 67 n.2) and Protarchus (21a–b) causes them to
fall into it, by claiming that the only good thing there is, is
pleasure: when dealing with two radically different objects, it
is easy to fall into the trap of polar thinking. Instead, Plato
points out that a life without both rationality and pleasure is
not a human life at all. This idea dictates the terms of the
examination of pleasure which follows: if there must be some
pleasures in the good life, a way to approach the nature of the
good life is to find out which pleasures are best. In effect – and
this is something Plato acknowledges at *Republic* 580d ff. – the
distinction of the kinds of ideal life is a division of the kinds of
pleasure which accompany these lives: sensual pleasures, pleasures found in being respected or pleasures found in intellectual activities.

It is easy enough to say what happens in the long examination of pleasure; it is less easy to say why it happens. Some
pleasures are found to deserve the attributes of truth and

purity, while others are condemned as false and mixed (impure). What does Plato mean by truth and falsity, purity and impurity, when these terms are applied to pleasures?

I PURE AND IMPURE PLEASURES

A pleasure is described as pure if it is unaccompanied by perceived pain; as impure if it is accompanied by pain. Plato's belief is that nearly all experiences of pleasure are in fact mixed experiences in which pain accompanies pleasure (50d). It follows that all such pleasures should be excluded from the good life since pain is by definition not desirable. The idea that most pleasures are accompanied by pain is argued for in 31b–36c and 44d–50e. The discussion is meant to be exhaustive in that it covers three types of mixed pleasures, which may be called 'physical', 'psycho-physical' and 'psychic', with the proviso that even physical sensations are psychic, given that the body by itself is insensitive (see 33d).

Physical Pleasures: 31d–32b, 46a–47c

The physical pleasures discussed in 31d–32b are not explicitly said to be mixed: the purpose of this part of the discussion is to establish a general model for pleasure. It follows from this general model that these and most other pleasures are mixed, and this is brought out in the case of physical pleasures in 46a–47c.

The general model is that pleasure is always remedial of a prior pain. This is ambiguous, but 44d ff. makes it clear that we should understand 'prior' not in the sense that at the onset of pleasure the pain vanishes. Rather, quenching thirst, for instance, is *only* pleasant because the thirst (the pain) is there to be quenched. Plato's confident assertion is: 'We'll never be able to examine pleasure adequately without also considering pain' (31b). One might query this confidence in his model. Having my back scratched, or walking in the country, are surely often pleasant without there having been any prior distress. It is difficult to see how they are restorations of some hypothetical natural state (31d) rather than disruptions of the state I was in beforehand. The strength of Plato's model is that it takes account of the relativity of sensations; the weakness is that it generalizes from too few examples.

Psycho-physical Pleasures: 33c–36c

These are the pleasures of anticipation. Some physical lack provokes the pleasure of anticipating the remedy to that lack. Again, these pleasures are not at the time said to be mixed, except roughly at 35e–36c; but they are referred to as mixed at 47c. It is clear in the latter passage that the body is involved, though formerly (32c, 33c) the pleasures were described as purely psychic: this is because in the earlier passage Plato is concentrating on the psychic element of what is later called a mixed experience. Nevertheless, the 'physical' pain which accompanies this type of pleasure is taken into account in 33c–35c, where the conditions of this type of pleasure are carefully explained. The complete picture is that a 'physical' lack leads to a desire to remedy the lack; desire involves memory coming into play to recollect what *will* remedy the lack; hence the mind anticipates the remedy.

Psychic Pleasures: 47d–50b

In this section Plato concentrates on spite, a painful psychic experience, to show that in his view it is in fact a mixture of pain and pleasure. We are meant to draw the same conclusion for all other purely psychic feelings, those in which pleasure predominates, as well as the painful ones that Plato enumerates.

Since this analysis of mixed pleasures covers nearly all the experiences we would normally call pleasant, the argument is in effect a *reductio ad absurdum* of hedonism. The hedonist wants to maximize both the quantity of his pleasures and their intensity, but on this analysis this means that he also wants to maximize the quantity and intensity of his pains (see 36d–e, 54e). Thus Plato stresses at 45a–c that intensity of pleasure depends on the degree of intensity of the accompanying pain.

Moreover, since pain is by definition not desirable, intense pleasures must be excluded from the good life whose ingredients must above all be desirable (20d, 60c). Another reason for their exclusion is given at 63d–e: once it has been established that knowledge is a necessary ingredient of the good life, intense pleasures have to be excluded because they would interrupt the mind at work. This is the point, familiar from the *Phaedo* and elsewhere, that the philosopher disdains intense pleasures.

If Plato is to abide consistently by this analysis of pleasure, how can he describe *any* pleasures as pure? He calls his solution to this dilemma an improvement (43b) on the original theory of the nature of pleasure. One might also call it a compromise: 20b–22b has shown that there must be *some* pleasures in the good life, but Plato has argued that *all* pleasures involve prior pain. Accordingly he postulates the existence of an intermediate state between pleasure and pain (42d–43d) which acts, as it were, as a buffer between the two. Thus relief from pain may not develop to the extent that the sensation becomes a positive pleasure: a slight motion may only get as far as this intermediate area and be mistakenly called pleasant only by contrast with the pain (43d–44a). Conversely, when the prior pain is so slight as to be imperceptible, the subsequent pleasure is not accompanied by any sensation of pain, and such a pleasure is therefore pure (51b). The examples Plato gives of such pure pleasures (51b–52b) show how uncommon he thinks their occurrence is: they are the pleasures found in the sight of simple geometrical forms and of pure colours, in the sound of single clear notes, in certain smells and last, but not least, in the acquisition of knowledge (provided that no prior or subsequent pain is involved).

The upshot of his consideration of pleasures as pure or impure is that only these unusual pleasures should be allowed in the good life since they are the only ones which do not contain the non-desirable element of pain. This is a rather inaccessible ideal. But later in the dialogue, in very vague language and entirely without warning (unless 12d counts as warning), another class of pleasures is allowed in. At 63e, in addition to pure pleasures, the 'pleasures which accompany virtue' are deemed to have a place in the good life. The context implies that these are *not* pure pleasures, and I have suggested (p. 143 n.4) that they are to be understood as minimally mixed. These pleasures are said to be 'necessary' to make the good life practicable (62e ff.), just as certain skills are necessary (62a ff.). Their domain, then, is probably meant to be the necessary everyday activities of eating, drinking, etc. (cf. *Republic* 558d ff.; Aristotle, *Nicomachean Ethics* 1147b 21 ff.), which must be present because without them life is impossible. The point, then, would be that if such activities are approached with virtue (self-control, etc.), they are consonant with the good life. Such pleasures would be minimally mixed in that, since I am virtuous, my self-control in resisting an extra portion of food is accompanied by hardly any regret at passing up the food. But all this is speculation: Plato chooses to leave us in the dark about how these pleasures fit in to his scheme. Is this one of the incomplete issues he mentions in the last words of the dialogue?

Nevertheless, the inclusion of pleasures which accompany virtue is understandable, even if not excusable in its vagueness. In the first place, it would be extremely odd for the virtues not to have a place in the good life and for the philosopher to be restricted to the pure pleasures described in 51b–52b. Secondly, I will later suggest that Plato's final recipe for the good life is built up from two triads of ideal and less ideal ingredients: under pressure from this schematic way of looking at things and from the grading of branches of knowledge (see p. 131 n.2), Plato includes these minimally mixed pleasures as the less ideal pleasures allowed into the good life.

II TRUE AND FALSE PLEASURES

It makes *prima facie* sense to describe a pleasure as pure or impure. It is more striking to describe it as true or false. Some of our surprise, however, may be dispelled by considering that, in Greek as in English, 'true' has a pre-logical, colloquial usage, in which it means 'real' or 'genuine'. But 'genuine' is a vague term: among other things it can imply 'actually existing' or 'honest' or 'not hybrid'. All these meanings will enter Plato's discussion of false pleasures, and it should be noticed from the start that there is a danger in this broadness: while 'hybrid' and 'dishonest' may be closely related, to say that something is false in these senses is far from saying that it is non-existent. Along with these colloquial senses of 'true' and 'false', we also find Plato trying out the application of a logical sense to some pleasures. As the metaphor of accuracy in 37d–e shows, the logical theory of truth which Plato takes for granted in the *Philebus*, as in other dialogues, is the one known as the correspondence theory of truth, whereby something is true if and only if it matches (corresponds to/with) the state of affairs it is meant to have as its object.

Bearing these matters in mind, let us turn to Plato's discussion of false pleasures in the *Philebus*. There are three sections, each discussing a different type of false pleasure: (*a*) 36c–40e; (*b*) 41a–42c; (*c*) 42c–44a.

[*a*] At 36c Socrates suggests that some pleasures of anticipation may be false. Protarchus disagrees; in his opinion all pleasures can only be true. Before turning to pleasures of anticipation themselves, Plato goes through some preliminaries which serve both to determine Protarchus' position and to set the stage for Socrates' attempt to refute him.

Protarchus' view that all pleasures are true is shown at 36e to be the view that all pleasures are genuine: any apparent case of pleasure is a genuine case. This is a plausible view, but ignores the possibility of self-deception: Socrates will explore some cases of self-deception. While insisting that pleasure is always true, Protarchus naturally admits that belief may be false as well as true. Socrates proceeds to develop an analogy between pleasure and belief (37a–e), which completes the preliminaries by adumbrating a weakness in Protarchus' position. The statement that all pleasures are true *qua* genuine fails to take account of the fact that some genuine beliefs are false: genuineness is not a sufficient condition of truth. While this point is not developed polemically straight away, we can see that it will enable Socrates to grant the genuineness of his first type of false pleasure, while also arguing for its falsity. The analogy is further developed to show the way in which Socrates will try to establish the falsity of pleasures of anticipation in this section (a), viz. the logical sense: they may fail to correspond with any external state of affairs.

The stage is now set and Socrates goes on to apply these preliminaries to the case of pleasures of anticipation. He will argue (i) that such pleasures may fail to correspond to the facts (37e–40c), and consequently (ii) that, even though genuine, such pleasures may be false (40c–e).

Plato argues that anticipatory pleasures may be false (or true) exactly as beliefs may be false (or true). At the same time, however, there is a closer relationship between false beliefs and false pleasures than merely one of analogy. It is true that some of the argument (37a–e, 40c–e) develops the analogy between pleasure and belief; but nevertheless at 37e Plato reveals that he is interested in cases where pleasure 'accompanies' false belief, and his own summary of the argument at 42a claims that the beliefs 'infect' the pleasures with falsity.

A considerable portion of the argument (38b–39e) is devoted to an analysis of how false belief arises. It is a belief which fails to correspond to a state of affairs: the state of affairs it affirms is a non-event or is not proper to that occasion. Such non-events may be anticipated, in which case we have false belief about the future. Beliefs, whether true or false, occur both as mental statements and as images. After going through this, Plato takes it as self-evident that pleasures which accompany false beliefs about the future are themselves false. When I believe that I will win the lottery when in fact I will not, not only my belief, but also the pleasure I currently experience while holding the belief, is false: its object is a non-event.

The notion of accompaniment needs spelling out, since it is not unimportant. Plato's idea, which is surely right, is that pleasure is not something separable from the activity which is being experienced as pleasant. It makes no sense to say 'I am walking in the country *and* I am having a pleasant experience', as if the pleasure could somehow be separated from the walking, taking in the scenery, etc., and attached to some other activity. Equally, there are times when the relevant 'activity' is a belief, and a prime example is belief about the future.

Despite this insight, however, one may still doubt whether Plato has proved his main thesis, that pleasure can be false exactly as belief can. A belief is false if it is mistaken in its object, but in the case of anticipated pleasure, it is not the *event* that is the object of the pleasure, but the 'accompanying' belief that the event will occur. Plato has not proved that the pleasure is mistaken in this object, and it is difficult to see how he could.

[*b*] The second type of false pleasures (41a–42c) need less commentary. I have explained the sort of situation Plato has in mind on p. 105 n. 1. He suggests that when, say, a present 'bodily' pain coincides with an anticipated pleasure, the size of both of them is distorted. Thus they are 'false' in the sense of 'dishonest', because they 'give an unreal impression'. So here Plato is no longer working with the logical sense of truth and falsity: the issue is not the occurrence or non-occurrence of the future event, but he is only concerned with the degree of intensity while the event is being anticipated. From a hypothetical objective standpoint, the experience is not 'true', though it is not denied that it is genuinely experienced.

[*c*] Plato introduces the third type of false pleasure (42c–44a) by establishing the existence of an intermediate state between pleasure and pain (42c–43d; see p. 20). Given this neutral state, it follows that some experiences thought to be pleasures are not pleasures at all, strictly speaking, but merely experiences of the neutral state which are thought to be pleasant by contrast with pain. Plato does not formally conclude the section with a statement that these 'pleasures' are false, but his meaning is plain enough (and see also *Republic* 584e–585a). At 42c he calls them even more false than the second type of false pleasures: this is presumably because it might be argued that the second type contain a core of non-illusory pleasure, whereas the third type are not even pleasures

in the first place. In this instance, then, 'false' means 'non-existent'.

We have seen that the three types of false pleasure are not all false in the same way. Plato moves with alarming ease from the logical to the colloquial senses of truth, and from one colloquial meaning to another: he could have made it clearer that 'truth' is being applied in different senses, especially since he begins by granting Protarchus' assumption that all pleasures are genuine, but later, with the third type of false pleasures, tacitly refutes it. To cap it all, we are soon told (52e–53c, especially) that pure pleasures are also true, in implicit contrast to some falsity that *mixed* pleasures have: this is yet another meaning of true and false, in which they mean 'non-hybrid' and 'hybrid' respectively. And this turns out to be a very pervasive sense of 'true': at 45a, with a reference back to 31e, he dismisses 'bodily' pleasures as hybrid, and at 47c, with a reference back to 36c, he dismisses the pleasures of anticipation as hybrid, before turning finally to the third type of mixed pleasures which he has not mentioned earlier in the dialogue. The result is that pure pleasures are contrasted with *all* the other pleasures which have been discussed, in respect not only of purity, but also of truth. Such a contrast is illegitimate, given that 'truth' has changed its meaning.

There is a curious loose end in this examination of pleasures in terms of truth and falsity. The maverick is the first type of false pleasures: ultimately we are told that they too are false in the sense of hybrid, as all mixed pleasures are; but initially they were called false by application of the logical standard of truth. As false in the sense of mixed or hybrid they are contrasted with the truth of pure pleasures; but as false in the logical sense, they are contrasted with the true pleasures of the good man's anticipation (40b–c). Now, these (logically) true pleasures are not the same as pure pleasures, since by the assertion of 47c even these logically true pleasures must be mixed. What are we to make of them? Why are they not included in the good life? They are, after all, true and the property of the good man and they accompany knowledge (38a). I suspect, though the text provides no certain guarantee of the correctness of this suspicion, that this loose end would have been tied up if Plato had tied up the other loose end of the 'pleasures which accompany virtue' (see pp. 20–21). It is likely that these logically true pleasures are a version of the pleasures which accompany virtue, and as such are allowed into the good life at the end of the dialogue. The virtue of the 'good man' of 39e ff. is explicit in his description as just and so on, and implicit in the modesty of his anticipations (see p. 101 n.2).

III CONCLUSIONS ABOUT HEDONISM

Plato's examination of pleasure concludes at 53c–55c with some remarks about those who take pleasure to be the goal in life. The first consideration (53c–54d) takes as its starting-point a theory about pleasure which Plato attributes to certain ingenious thinkers. Plato agrees with their view, or at least with the conclusion their view necessitates, which is that pleasure cannot be the ultimate goal. It is only the means to some end, so if you pursue pleasure, you are not pursuing a genuine goal.

This consideration presumably applies to *all* pleasures, pure and impure, so how can Plato reconcile it with his previous evaluation of pleasures? The answer is that in the Platonic good life, certain pleasures *are* allowed, but they are not the goal. The goal is knowledge, and those pleasures are permitted which do not impede the mind (63d–64a). So even these admissible pleasures remain a means to the goal of knowledge.

Plato next (54e–55a) connects this view of pleasure with his own view of the nature of pleasure as explained earlier in the dialogue. The ingenious thinkers show that hedonism is absurd, and Plato supports this by saying that if pleasure is always remedial of pain, the pursuit of pleasure entails the pursuit of pain: hedonism is self-contradictory. He expresses this point in terms of sensual pleasure, presumably because, since they are the most intense, they best illustrate the point; but the idea holds good, given Plato's theory of pleasure, for the pursuit of any mixed pleasures, not just sensual ones.

Finally he adds a paragraph (55b–c) which is not so much a direct refutation of hedonism, as a challenge: it suggests the enormity of the task the hedonist faces. He must prove (i) that goodness is only a property of the soul; since pleasure is a psychic experience (33c ff.), the hedonist must claim that purely physical properties, such as beauty (which the Greeks commonly held to be a good thing), do not deserve the title 'good'; (ii) that no other psychic property besides pleasure deserves to be called good; (iii) that every time the words 'good', 'better' and 'best' are used, they can sensibly be supplanted by 'pleasant', 'more pleasant' and 'most pleasant'. It is not known whether this challenge was ever taken up directly: hedonists such as Eudoxus, Aristippus and Epicurus do not seem to have argued in precisely these terms.

IV THE EXAMINATION OF KNOWLEDGE

The examination of knowledge (55c–59d) proceeds by grading branches of knowledge in terms of their truth, purity and precision. These three criteria are equivalent: purity is to be glossed as 'freedom from irrational elements such as guesswork, i.e. involvement with precise methods and precise objects'. A branch of knowledge is pure if it is uncontaminated by its opposite, guesswork, just as a pleasure is pure if it is uncontaminated by its opposite, pain. Equally, freedom from guesswork makes a branch of knowledge true and precise, i.e. a more exact science. At the same time the objects of branches of knowledge, however immaterial they may be, are graded in terms of truth and precision. In Platonic metaphysics the most true objects are immaterial: they are not liable to the inconstancy and change which characterizes the physical world. So a true branch of knowledge, one which fully deserves the title, is one which uses precise methods and focuses on precise objects. During the grading, however, Plato sometimes concentrates on method as the criterion, sometimes on the objects.

He begins by distinguishing between 'practical' and 'educational' branches of knowledge. It is not clear what we are to make of this distinction. It could be that *all* the branches of knowledge to be distinguished are thought to belong to the practical side: Plato starts with this half of the division and never signals a change to the other half. But it is rather awkward to see some of the higher branches of knowledge as practical, whereas they fit well under the heading of educational: it is probable that at a certain point in the grading Plato switches from the practical kind to the educational kind. It would then follow that the educational branches of knowledge are more precise than the practical ones. This does not conflict with Platonic theory: if the practical sciences deal with the material world, and the educational kind with the world of thought, he would be inclined to think of the latter as more precise.

The course of the grading of branches of knowledge is slightly tortuous: in addition to a straightforward linear gradation, Plato makes a lateral move as well. This will become clear as we consider the passage. He starts with a division of the practical branches of knowledge. *All* practical branches of knowledge contain *some* degree of reliance on mathematics, otherwise they would not be branches of knowledge in the first place; but some contain more than others. Music-making is a prime example of a skill which is 'full of guesswork', i.e. short on mathematics. For instance, in playing a stringed instrument, you do not actually get out a ruler and measure where to put your finger. It is somewhat unfair of Plato to concentrate on stringed instruments, since it is easily arguable that in playing a wind instrument the measuring has been done for you in advance by the craftsman who bored the holes in the right place. But Plato's point would still be that little actual mathematics takes place during music-making. At 56b he reveals that he wants us to think the same way about 'medicine, farming, helmsmanship and military command': the reason why these are to be counted as imprecise branches of knowledge will become clear shortly. It is worth bearing in mind that music-making is imprecise not just in method but because, at

28

least in playing stringed instruments, the objects – the strings – are moving (56a): they do not afford the sort of constancy which enhances precision. These imprecise practical branches of knowledge are contrasted with building, which Plato takes as the prime example of a more precise practical science. Its greater precision is said to be due to its method: it uses accurate tools.

We now come to what I earlier called the lateral move in the argument. Mathematics is agreed to be the next stage in the linear gradation (56c), but this agreement is qualified by dividing it (56d – 57e) into 'common' (applied) and 'philosophical' (pure) mathematics. It turns out that philosophical mathematics is the next *linear* stage, whereas the common variety is distinguished *laterally*: common mathematics is no more than an alternative description of both the kinds of practical science which have just been distinguished. This is clear enough from how the common kind of mathematics is described at 56d: the distinction between the two varieties is made on the basis of the precision of their objects, and the objects of common mathematics are said to include armies and cows. These must be the objects of military command and farming respectively, which were included at 56b among the most imprecise branches of knowledge. Moreover, at 56e, building too is distinguished from philosophical mathematics. So common mathematics turns out to be a blanket term for both the kinds of practical sciences.

Nevertheless, there is a tension here in that sometimes (at 57c–d especially) Plato talks as if common and philosophical mathematics were the next *two* linear stages after building and related sciences. I take it that this is only a tension, not an inconsistency, and that we are faced here only with different points of view. From one point of view common mathematics is theoretically separable, since it is that which all practical sciences *use*; from another point of view it is not separable since all sciences, to be sciences, i.e. to be located in Plato's hierarchy of branches of knowledge in the first place, must use some mathematics (55e). If common mathematics were in fact separable from the practical sciences, as a distinct branch of knowledge, that would be to deny them any scientific status at all. From the former point of view, but not from the latter, it will be convenient to talk as if common mathematics were a further linear stage. But from both points of view it remains true *in fact* that common mathematics is a description of the scientific element of the practical sciences.

The objects of philosophical mathematics are abstract and therefore more exact than cows, wood and stone. It is here, I suggest, that we move from practical branches of knowledge to the educational kind. When we teach a child that two plus two makes four, we are not dealing with cows and bricks (though we may use these as illustrations), but with the bare numbers that can be applied to cows and bricks. Many philosophers, including Plato, have held that the knowledge that two plus two makes four is *a priori* knowledge, that is, knowledge of something that is independent of the data of the physical world.

The next, and final, stage of the linear division is the distinction of dialectic. 'Dialectic' is Plato's standard word for what a philosopher does. Its root is the Greek verb meaning 'to converse' (as in the philosophical conversations of Socrates); the purpose of such conversations is to find out 'what each thing is' (*Republic* 533b). Hence the word came to mean 'the discovery and knowledge of the truth about things', and this is the province of the philosopher. The view assumed in the *Philebus* and expounded more fully in the *Phaedo* and *Republic* is that the true nature of things is not determined by their physical nature, but by their participation in another, immaterial world inhabited by what Plato calls Forms. The Forms are the true nature of things: an action is just, for instance, because it partakes of the Form of Justice. These Forms are each immaterial, uniform and unchanging, and as such are the most precise objects of knowledge, and dialectic is accordingly the most precise branch of knowledge.

After a digression about rhetoric (58b–d), Protarchus comes

round to Socrates' view that dialectic is the acme of knowledge. This conclusion is expressed (58e–59a) by saying that 'most other sciences' deal merely with the physical world, and that their mental faculty is 'belief' rather than knowledge. Again this presupposes the fuller treatment of the *Republic*, where Plato proposes that, strictly speaking, the term 'knowledge' should be reserved for dialectic, and that the nature of the physical world is such that one can only have beliefs about it.

The position of philosophical mathematics is unclear in this context. On the one hand its objects are not of this world, but on the other hand Plato does not expressly put it on a par with dialectic. Again it is helpful to turn to the *Republic* where Plato explains his position on this issue. At *Republic* 511a Plato contrasts pure mathematics with dialectic in terms of method: as far as their objects are concerned, they are probably on a par, but whereas dialectic operates entirely within the intelligible world, mathematics uses sensible objects (e.g. geometrical diagrams) to draw conclusions about the intelligible world. It is therefore an inferior form of knowledge. The reason that philosophical mathematics has effectively dropped out of the discussion in the *Philebus* must be that Plato does not want to cover the same ground as in the *Republic*.

The final scheme of the *Philebus*, which is arguably similar to the famous Divided Line of *Republic* 509d–511e, is as follows:

A	B	C	D
e.g. music	e.g. building	philosophical mathematics	dialectic

A + B = practical branches of knowledge; common
  mathematics
C + D = educational branches of knowledge
A + B = belief, having this world as its object
C + D = knowledge, having the world of Forms as its
  object.

V THE GOOD LIFE

Plato's examination of pleasure and knowledge is complete and he can begin to construct the good life. Since we know, from 20c–22c (recapitulated at 60b–61a), that any human life must consist of both pleasure and reason, then both must be included. But since the issue is not *any* human life, but the best one, it has been necessary to discover which are the best (purest/truest) kinds of pleasure and knowledge. The discussion which establishes the ingredients of the good life is easy enough to follow (61d–64a): the obvious starting-point is to include pure pleasures and dialectic but, while this may be an ideal, it is acknowledged to be inaccessible, with the result that less ideal members of each class are allowed in. These are *all* the other branches of knowledge, and the minimally mixed pleasures which accompany virtue.

What is less easy to follow is 64a–66d. The dialogue is in effect complete before this appendix, but Plato wants to set his conclusion in an abstract context. Earlier in the dialogue (22c ff.) the following question had been raised: even if both pleasure and reason must be present in the good life, which of them causes the goodness of the good life? This is taken to be the way to establish their relative priority. At 64d Plato raises the question again, in order to settle it in the context of the actual life that is being recommended.

The way in which he answers the question is to reduce the goodness of the good life to three separate properties – truth, moderation (or proportion) and beauty – and to argue that reason has more affinity than pleasure to these three properties. It is reason that is truthful, moderate and beautiful; therefore the fact that the good life is characterized by these three properties must be due to the presence of reason, not pleasure. The argument is unsatisfactory in its dogmatism: of the three properties, we get argument, rather than bare assertion, only for moderation as a feature of the good life; and it needs to be made clearer that the meanings of truth, beauty and moderation are the same when it is said that the good life has them, that reason has them, and that pleasure fails to have them. The whole discussion relies too much on the persuasive power of abstract terms like beauty and truth.

There is another mistake running through the discussion. As the argument about moderation shows (64d–e), it is a feature of the good life *qua* a mixture (of the ingredients decided on in 61d–64a). Yet the argument which deprives pleasure of affinity with the three properties concentrates on intense, and especially sensual, pleasures (65c–66a), which are *not* included in the mixture. In other words it has not been shown that the sorts of pleasures which are allowed in the good life do not possess these properties and are not responsible for the goodness of the good life: indeed, at 52c, pure pleasures are expressly said to be moderate. Rather than debating whether pleasure *or* reason provides the goodness of the good life, it would surely have been more true to Plato's position for him to claim that the good life possesses these properties because it is a mixture of just these rational faculties and just these pleasures.

By 65a a shift has occurred in the terms of the argument. Rather than simply establishing the superiority of reason over pleasure on the basis of its greater responsibility for the goodness of the good life, which is what the whole of the dialogue has led us to expect, it is said that the three properties of the good mixture are themselves responsible for the goodness of the good life. Consequently, when at 66a Plato orders the things responsible for the goodness of the good life, he places these properties above both reason and pleasure. This makes the list somewhat peculiar: how can properties sensibly be *compared* to the things that possess them? The objection is anachronistic, however. Greek philosophers before Aristotle had not clearly distinguished between substances and properties: if water changed from hot to cold, it was thought to lose the hot substance and gain the cold. In this way, despite the theory of Forms (p. 30) which might have enabled him fully to distinguish properties and substances, Plato includes beauty, etc., as substantial ingredients of the good life along with pleasure and reason.

Plato's concluding list has a further peculiarity, which is less easy to explain. The list is this (66a−c):

1. Moderation, order and so on.
2. Proportion, beauty, perfection, sufficiency and so on.
3. Intellect and reason (i.e. dialectic; see 59d).
4. Other branches of knowledge.
5. Pure pleasures.
6. Other necessary pleasures (see pp. 20−21).

The preceding discussion has led us to expect at most a three-part list: the properties, reason, pleasure. Suddenly we are faced with a list with six members. Why is the list doubled? In particular, why is moderation distinguished from proportion, when they have consistently been identified in the preceding discussion? Plato provides us with no explicit grounds for answering the question, but it is possible to speculate that the reason is as follows.

The rationale of the reduplication of reason and pleasure is easy to discern: the third and fifth places are occupied by those aspects of each which we might call ideal, the fourth and sixth by those which are only included in the good life because of some necessity (see 62a−d on necessary branches of knowledge; 63e [cf. 62e] on necessary pleasures). This consideration can, I believe, also explain why the properties are split between the first two stages of the list, when they have been consistently identified before.

It will clarify my interpretation, though it is not necessary to it, if we suppose that here, as elsewhere in the dialogues, Plato originally accompanied the text with a diagram. The simplest diagrammatic representation of the interpretation I am suggesting is as follows:

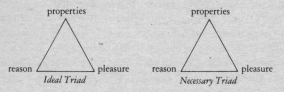

properties
reason   pleasure
Ideal Triad

properties
reason   pleasure
Necessary Triad

This displays both the essential triadic nature of the good life, and the reduplication of the three into six. The repetition of the properties is now understandable: both the ideal and the less ideal ingredients must be related in such a way that these properties obtain, otherwise they cannot be the ingredients of the *good* life. At the same time the straightforward hierarchy from 1 to 6 makes sense: reason in all its manifestations must precede pleasure (65a–66a), and the properties must precede both reason and pleasure (65a). A writer who had a more sophisticated system of numeration than was available to Plato would no doubt have written the hierarchy as 1(a), 1(b), 2(a) . . . 3(b), where (a) refers to the ideal triad and (b) to the necessary triad.

It might be wondered why dialectic and pure pleasures are suitable companions in the ideal triad, and the other branches of knowledge are accompanied by the minimally mixed pleasures in the less ideal triad. Each pair is perfectly matched in Platonic theory. One of the essential distinctions Plato saw between knowledge and belief is that knowledge is always true, whereas belief can be either true or false. So in the *Philebus* knowledge is accompanied by those pleasures which are always true, and the other branches of knowledge, whose mental faculty is belief (58e–59a), are accompanied by pleasures which can be either true or false. In the good life, however, both belief and the minimally mixed pleasures must be true: 66b (cf. 11b) specifies that these branches of knowledge must be true, and see pp. 25–6 for pleasures which accompany virtue as true.

So ends the contribution of the *Philebus* to the ethical debate of Plato's day: the rest of the dialogue merely recapitulates the course of the discussion. It will be convenient to summarize his conclusions in the context of the pursuit of *eudaimonia*. *Eudaimonia*, commonly translated 'happiness', is the Greek word for whatever condition a person thinks is worth aiming for: a hedonist, then, would say that pleasure is or provides *eudaimonia*. The word does not occur often in the *Philebus*: only at 11d and 47b in this ethical sense, where I have translated it as 'what fulfils a man', because 'happiness' may have hedonistic overtones in the first place. Despite the rarity of its occurrence, it pervades the dialogue in that it is agreed at the outset (11d–e) that the purpose of the conversation is to see whether pleasure, reason or 'some third state' (i.e. a combination of pleasure and reason) provides *eudaimonia* for man.

Plato's conclusion, then, is as follows. Man, *qua* man and not animal (animals are purely sensual) nor god (gods are purely intellectual), can only be *fulfilled* by some combination of pleasure and reason. But not *any* combination. Man does have the divine spark of reason and capacity for (philosophical) knowledge within himself; therefore the fulfilment of man will be the maximization of this potential. This rational side of man is hindered by intense pleasures, so these must be excluded: in any case they are mixed with pain. Moreover certain pleasures are found with false beliefs (all the types of false pleasures are accompanied by false belief of some kind or another), which obviously do not allow man to realize his capacity for knowledge, which is always true. But this is not to say that all pleasures can be excluded: man has his sensual side too, to deny which would be to deny his nature. But this sensual side, the desire for pleasure, must be subordinated to the rational, which of all the animals is man's property alone. Therefore those pleasures which really contribute to man's *eudaimonia* are those which accompany and/or do not hinder his pursuit of knowledge (and his practice of the cardinal virtues).

Basically, then, it is a belief (assumed rather than argued for) about man's nature which leads Plato to his conclusions about man's *eudaimonia*. It is arguable, though this is not the place to pursue such a claim, that the conclusions of the *Philebus* do not substantially conflict with his recommendations in other dialogues. The *Philebus*, as Plato's most deliberate and thorough attempt to describe the good life, may be regarded as the canonical Platonic text on the subject of the way men ought to live.

METHOD AND METAPHYSICS

It is one of the most remarkable features of the *Philebus* that we have been able to discuss its ethical doctrines without a single reference to the methodological and metaphysical passages of the dialogue (12b–19a, 23b–31b). For this reason, and because a satisfactory discussion of these complex and important passages is necessarily beyond the scope of this Introduction, I shall consider them only so far as is necessary to answer the question: why did Plato include them in the dialogue? The earlier passage is expressly signalled by Plato as a digression (20b–c), so we need not look for any connection between it and the ethical issues as developed in the rest of the dialogue. But the later metaphysical passage, 23b–31b, is said at 23b–c to be related to what has preceded it, and it is suggested at 31c, 41d and 52c that it is relevant to the rest of the dialogue as well.

I SCIENTIFIC ANALYSIS

The discussion of methodology (16c–19a) is a natural development of the preliminary discussion (11a–16b). The issue of the dialogue is established at 11d–12a to be whether reason, pleasure or 'some other condition of the soul' is the good for man. The possibility that neither reason nor pleasure is the good, however, is shelved until 20b ff., when it turns out that the mixture of them both is better than either of them in isolation. This idea then dictates the course of the rest of the dialogue, but up until this point the presupposition is that pleasure and reason are to be considered in isolation.

The hedonist thesis that Protarchus adopts is that pleasure is the good. At 12c ff. Socrates suggests that such a position is too simplistic: the bare formulation implies that man should pursue *all* pleasures, but might it not be the case that we should make a preliminary distinction between pleasures which are worth having and those which are not? Protarchus resists this suggestion, as he must if he is to be consistent, because it would deprive pleasure of being the factor that decides goodness: instead we would have to consider pleasure merely as an accessory to some other state, e.g. wisdom or folly (12c–d) and the goodness of the whole experience would be decided not by the element of pleasure, but by whether wisdom or foolishness was good or bad.

The point Socrates is trying to get across is that although Protarchus is undoubtedly right to insist that all pleasures are somehow similar, *qua* pleasant, it still makes sense to ask whether there are differences within that unity. This is expressed in a typically Platonic way, as if the single nature of all instances of pleasure was a separately identifiable entity which all the instances somehow share, while also having specific differences from one another. Interestingly, this is a development of the situation we find in the earliest dialogues, where it is Socrates, rather than the interlocutor, who insists on the unity of the subject of the discussion. Here Socrates takes the unity for granted, and emphasizes the differences within the unity.

The argument is curiously incomplete and dogmatic. At 13a Socrates suggests that if Protarchus agrees to there being differences between pleasures, he will also have to agree to expressing this difference in terms of the goodness and badness of pleasures. This does not follow at all: Protarchus could agree that pleasures are different but still claim that they are all good or worth having. Plato could have made plainer the point, mentioned above, that the acknowledgement of differences between pleasures will necessitate the consideration of the goodness or badness of the activity which pleasure accompanies, rather than merely noting the occurrence of pleasure and calling it good. The issue here is the nature of pleasure: it is not, says Plato implicitly, something separable from the activity (see also pp. 23–4), so that one can say that *whatever* pleasure accompanies, the pleasure itself is good. Rather pleasure is something supervenient on an activity, so that its goodness or badness is determined by the goodness or badness of the activity. However Plato never explicitly develops a theory of the nature of pleasure in these terms: he seems rather to be taking it for granted, in the sense that this seems to him to be the case, but he has not fully articulated *what* seems to him to be the case – this is the condition of most men on most subjects. Had he articulated it, Socrates' argument against Protarchus would have been strengthened.

The situation by 13c, then, is that due to the dogmatism of Socrates' argument, Protarchus refuses to acknowledge any differences between pleasures. However he is soon won round by the extraordinarily trivial device of Socrates acknowledging that there are differences between branches of his own candidate, knowledge. Socrates thinks they can now proceed to see whether pleasure or knowledge is the good. In other words, Protarchus' final position is this: all cases of pleasure are pleasant, though there may be other relevant factors which determine differences between them; but insofar as they are pleasant, they are all good. This is the position the dialogue sets out to combat.

One might expect Socrates to begin now to show how different types of pleasure (and different branches of knowledge) may be good or bad. Instead he goes off at a different tack, which is not immediately relevant to the ethical issue of the dialogue. He points out that what underlies the preceding discussion is the general problem of how *anything* can be simultaneously 'one and many'. Two forms of one-and-many problems are mentioned but dismissed as irrelevant for the current inquiry (14c–e). The one Plato is interested in is how any single concept or Form, e.g. Man or Pleasure, can have many instances (15a–b). He points out (15d–16a) that everyday speech tends to obscure the fact that the many instances of a concept are different from one another, by making it sound as though the relation of any instance to the single concept is all that matters. He proposes (16b–17a) and then illustrates (17a–18d) a method of analysis, which avoids the dangers of everyday speech.

Even if the passage is a digression, the flow of the discussion is natural, and the issues are important enough to justify their inclusion: it is obviously important not to overlook the differences that obtain even between similar objects, and the proposal of a scheme to account for both the similarities and the differences is ambitious. Three questions arise for the present study: (1) What is this scheme of analysis? (2) How is it meant to answer the questions of 15b? (3) How is it meant to be applied to the ethical issues of the dialogue, in particular to Protarchus' position on pleasure?

[1] The process of analysis is outlined in 16b–17a in a way which Plato admits is obscure and so he provides examples (17a–18d). Essentially, the argument is that a *scientific* procedure must take account not only of the indefinite plurality of instances of any single concept or phenomenon, but also of the definite number of types or varieties that these instances fall under. This is illustrated in the case of the phenomena of human speech and musical sound. Human speech is a single thing, consisting of an indefinite number of applications of letters, but there are a limited number of letters in the alphabet. The example of musical sound is less readily comprehensible, but Plato seems to assume that there are a limited number of ways in which notes can combine to form 'systems'. We know little of Greek musicology in Plato's time, but what he says here squares with the theory of Aristoxenus (born c. 370). Musical systems were built up from tetrachords either in conjunction (i.e. two tetrachords making seven notes) or disjunction (eight notes). Thus the so-called Greater Perfect System consists of two pairs of conjunct tetrachords plus an extra note (fifteen notes in all). Within this system the Greeks distinguished seven different modes each consisting of an octave but starting from a different note in the system. So Plato would be saying that scientific musicology knows the tetrachords, and the systems and modes which are based on them.

It is noticeable that Plato chooses to illustrate the scientific method he is recommending in its application to sensible phenomena. At the same time, however, he believes that it can be applied to immaterial concepts such as pleasure, goodness, humanity, etc. It is interesting to note the wide-ranging nature of the scientific method proposed: the generality of the discussion is such that it can accomodate any particular method of analysis, or any sort of object, provided only that the method takes account of the 'intermediates'.

In other dialogues, notably the *Sophist* and *Politicus*, Plato recommends and displays a process which does this in the case of concepts: a genus is divided into species and so on down to the *infimae species*. Presumably he has this in mind in the *Philebus* for dealing with concepts, although it is not developed. A genus (the 'original One') is divided into the appropriate number of species, each of which is similarly divided, and so on until no further specific differences are taken to be relevant, that is, until one reaches the *infimae species*. At this point 'each of all the units can be dismissed and released into the indeterminate' (16e): after this point no further conceptual divisions are made and it is simply acknowledged that there are, potentially or actually, indefinitely many instances of the concept in question.

[2] At 15b Plato formulates a question about the relation of a concept or Form to its instances in the physical world. This is indeed an important question for Plato to consider, and one which he discusses at length in the first part of the *Parmenides*. In other dialogues he had resorted to metaphor, saying that the particular instances 'partake of' or 'imitate' the Form. Both metaphors imply two properties for Forms: first, that they are objective entities, which are there to be partaken of or imitated; and second that while particulars depend for their existence on Forms, Forms do not depend on particulars – there could be a Form of something which has no physical embodiment, like unicorns.

As long as Plato persists in seeing Forms as independently existing entities, the question of their relation to their embodiments arises, and is an important one for Plato to answer. Aristotle, while still adopting the 'realist' position that universals have a real existence, adopted the more reasonable view that the question of the relation of universals to things is an empty question: universals stand to particulars as an impression does to the wax in which it is impressed. Just as it is impossible for an impression to exist without wax, so it is impossible for universals to exist without particulars: it is pointless to see the relation as something added on to a separately existing entity.

In the *Philebus* Plato implies that the method of scientific analysis will help answer this question. But the way in which he expresses himself in 16c−17a precludes any definite answer. Division of Forms down to the *infimae species* is still division into Forms and sub-Forms, and cannot tell us anything about the relation of Forms and particulars. It will enable us to classify particulars into groups falling under this or that sub-Form as well as the generic Form, but it cannot help us spell out what 'fall under' means. It would be most charitable to Plato to suppose that he means us to understand that the method of scientific analysis is a *preliminary* to answering the question of 15b, rather than that it automatically does so.

[3] At 18d−19a Plato claims that a scientific approach to pleasure and knowledge will determine the question of their relative priority. Again, it is difficult to see how this is so. Clearly, a complete classification of types of pleasure will undermine Protarchus' confidence in the unity of all pleasures *qua* pleasant, and it may even enable him to see that some pleasures are preferable to others. But where do we go from there? Are we supposed, perhaps, to add up the number of 'good' pleasures and 'good' branches of knowledge, and find that the number of the latter exceeds that of the former? This would be absurd. It seems that while Plato envisages a fully scientific analysis of pleasure and knowledge, he is (i) unwilling or unable to provide it − hence we find the more informal classification in the rest of the dialogue; and (ii) unclear on how this will help the ethical issue of the dialogue.

In answer to our question − what part does 12b−19a play in the dialogue? − we can only say that it acts as a prospectus. The best way to solve the ethical issues, Plato suggests, is by applying the scientific method. Although this suggestion is not fulfilled by Plato himself, it is valuable as a counteragent to the tendency, which is liable to accompany hedonism, to approach life thoughtlessly, flitting from one pleasure to the next. Many will feel that the Platonic ultra-rational approach is just as unpalatable, but it is typical of Plato that he sees the way one ought to live as a subject capable of rational treatment.

II METAPHYSICS: 23B–31B

This is undoubtedly the most troublesome section of the dialogue: it is difficult to understand both in itself and in its connections with the rest of the dialogue. It opens with the dramatic and sweeping statement that there are in the universe only four kinds of things, which are called *limit, indeterminacy*, the *result* of mixing these two, and the *cause* of their mixing (23c–d). We are plunged immediately into that aspect of ancient (and medieval) philosophy which is most alien to modern tastes; we tend to be wary of such grand schemes.

I propose first to discuss the ethical purpose of this piece of metaphysics, before turning to a few of the many problems of interpretation. The ethical purpose of the passage is supposed to consist in its provision of a metaphysical justification of the ethical recommendations of the dialogue: if *everything* in the universe is covered by this scheme, then the good life and its ingredients are no exceptions.

The first hint of an ethical purpose arises in relation to the immediately preceding argument, 20c–23a. We have just been told that the good life is a *mixed* life (22d), i.e. consisting of both pleasure and reason, and the question has been raised about which of these two ingredients is *responsible* for the goodness of the good life. Then, at the start of our section, we come across the same terms, mixture and responsibility (the Greek word for 'cause' being the same as that for 'responsible'). It turns out that the good life belongs to the mixed class (27d), reason is a cause (28c–31a), and pleasure is an indeterminate (27e, 31a). The idea is that, like all causes, reason imposes limit on what is indeterminate, i.e. that it restrains the proliferation of pleasure.

Now, this is very neat, and there are echoes at the end of the dialogue when the question of responsibility resurfaces (see p. 32 ff.). We must ask, however, whether the ethical ideas fit as neatly into the metaphysical scheme as Plato intends. It is suggested at 22d and confirmed at 64c ff. that reason is responsible for the goodness of the good life. But causes in the metaphysical scheme are responsible for mixing. The two sorts of responsibility can only be paired either if any and every 'mixed' thing is good, or if *some* causes, e.g. the elevated faculties of human and divine minds, cause good mixtures, while other lesser faculties cause less good mixtures. Probably this latter idea is what Plato has in mind, since although in 25e ff. the examples he chooses of mixed things are all good, yet elsewhere we find that some mixed things are neutral at least: any living organism (32b) and any human life (20c–23a). If Plato's idea is to distinguish in this way between better and worse rational faculties, it is a pity he did not express it more clearly.

Apart from the ethical purpose of this section, the most explicit connection drawn is between it and the earlier discussion of scientific method (16–18). At 23b Plato suggests that there 'may be some overlap' between the terms or substance of the two passages; specifically, we find a few lines further on that the overlap is supposed to consist of identity in the use of the terms 'limit' and 'indeterminate', which are now being taken to be two of the four kinds of thing which exhaust the whole world. Obviously, however, nothing was said explicitly in 16–18 about such categories, so we must pursue Plato's claim further, to see what he might mean. It is necessary first to give some interpretation of the metaphysics of 23–31.

The interpretation that I wish to suggest of this passage is one that used to be dominant but has recently come under fire. According to this view, three of Plato's four 'classes' are forerunners of three of Aristotle's four causes. The 'cause' is the efficient cause, 'indeterminate' is akin to the material cause, and 'limit' to the formal cause. On Aristotelian lines, this pencil is a mixed thing, one might say, produced by the pencil-maker (the efficient cause) out of wood, graphite, etc. (the material cause) which has had a certain shape and form imposed on it (the formal cause).

We read in 26c–27b, which is the clearest passage in an otherwise opaque section, that the mixed class consists of things that are generated, and we already know from 15a–b (and many other passages in the dialogues) that this is the way that Plato describes the physical world. It has been doubted whether we ought to conclude that the mixed class consists solely of physical things because the examples Plato gives of the mixed class are things like health and the good life, which are types of thing rather than particular things; so is he not analysing universals, either solely or as well as particulars? I think not: Plato would never describe universals as generated, which is what the mixed class explicitly is. His use of general terms like health is still comprehensible within the context of an analysis of particulars. There is a perfectly ordinary use of general terms in which they mean 'any and every instance of . . .' 'Health is a proper balance of the humours' can mean 'any instance of health is a proper balance of the humours'.

We also read in 26c–27b that the indeterminate and limit are the elements of the mixed class: physical things are a product of the mixture of indeterminates and limit, the mixing being undertaken by a cause, which must in all cases be mind (either God's or some person's). We are told in 24a–25a that *in itself* the indeterminate changes and increases continually. This would be an extraordinary assertion if we were meant to locate certain identifiable things of the world in this class, because nothing in the world is like this: it may be possible to run the mile in three and a half minutes, but it will never be possible to do so in thirty seconds. For Plato this is because, apart from the principle of expansion, there is also the principle of limitation, which is described in 25a–b in terms of mathematical precision. Plato's conviction that the world does have order in it is clearly expressed in 28–31.

So 24a–25a is a description of indeterminacy in essence. At 26a–b Plato talks of climatic conditions as the product of imposing limit on wintry storms, and so on for other cases. Wintry storms are clearly the indeterminate element, but according to my interpretation, as particular things, they should belong to the mixed class. Plato, I think, would agree that these things *do* belong to the mixed class, because there can never be a wintry storm which gets unceasingly colder and windier. The point is that wintry storms are potentially or essentially like this, even if never actually, so they are a suitable indeterminate element. A case in point is pleasure, which we are told is the indeterminate element in human life. This entails (31a) that *in itself* pleasure has 'no beginning, middle or end'. But clearly life, fortunately, does not consist of unending increasing pleasure: pleasure is limited (see 21a–22b).

A final problem to be considered is that the mixed things Plato mentions within this passage are all good: health, beauty and so on. Perhaps all mixed things are good, in which case it is wrong to locate all particular instances, good, bad and indifferent, in this class: perhaps particulars which are not good should be located in the indeterminate class. I have already suggested (p. 44) that indifferent things are explicitly located in the mixed class, and (in the preceding paragraph) that we ought to see even 'bad' things here too, if wintry storms are bad. There is further evidence of the correctness of these conclusions. In the first place it is worth noting the generality of statements such as '[the combination of limit and indeterminacy] results in each case in the production of things' (25e). Secondly, given Plato's conviction of the essential orderliness of the universe, as expressed particularly in the assertion that 'there is *sufficient* limit' (30e), it should follow that nothing is utterly indeterminate, though some things may be more so than others. Thirdly, notice the emphasis in 25e–26a that *proper* integration produces good results, the implication being that some combinations, while still being combinations, are less fortunate.

We can now consider the connection of this passage with
16–18. I take it that when Plato talks of overlap between the
two passages he means us to think along the following lines.
The metaphysics concerns the creation of things, whereas
scientific method leads to the discovery of order within the
disorder of things. This is a difference, but still the creative
mind is a skilful or scientific mind, so there must be some
similarity to science as described before (the word translated
'fashion' in 27b is a verb for 'work with skill or science' and,
incidentally, is cognate with Plato's famous Demiurge or
Craftsman of the *Timaeus*). So just as Theuth (18b ff.) imposes order on disorder, the creative mind creates by check-
ing the expansion of indeterminacy. Indeterminacy is applied
to different things in the two passages, but has much the
same meaning. In 16–18 the quantitative and qualitative indeterminacy of all letters, for example, is limited by the discovery of similarities, so that sets of similar letters (vowels,
etc.) are found, and ultimately the alphabet is formed. In 23
–6 qualitative indeterminacy is limited in that 'hotter' implies no fixed point on the quality-range of heat. Indeterminacy refers to particulars in 16–18, but not in 23–6; but
this is a difference of reference, not of meaning, of the term
'indeterminate'.

Despite this degree of overlap, however, Plato's words at
23b–c are still misleading, given the difference of reference
just mentioned. It would have been less misleading if Plato
had used different terms, to avoid the implication that particulars are the members of the class of indeterminates in
23 ff. In 16–18 *everything* has indeterminacy in it: equality,
for instance, has indeterminately many instances of different
types. But in the language of 23 ff. equality is specifically
not indeterminate. As we have seen, in 23 ff., 'indeterminate' does not refer primarily to things at all, but rather to factors within things. Nor could Plato reasonably claim that in
23 ff. he is extrapolating from the indeterminacy of particulars in 16–18, because the primary sense of indeterminacy in
16–18 is quantitative.

Finally, what use is made of this piece of metaphysics in the rest of the dialogue? At 41d and 52c, during the analysis of pleasure, the indeterminacy of pleasure is expressly mentioned, but it is clear that in both cases the mention is gratuitous: for instance, at 41d Plato need only have said that the pleasures in question are difficult to assess, without attributing this to the general indeterminacy of pleasure. The same goes for the reference to the mixed class at 31c: the theory of the origin and nature of pleasure stands or falls on its own without this reference. These passing references look like attempts to tie the metaphysics in to the rest of the dialogue, when it is really a digression from the main ethical issues, like 16–18. While it is possible to be critical of the formal appropriateness of including these passages in the dialogue, it must be remembered that Plato was rarely the kind of philosophical writer who tackles a single thesis and its ramifications without allowing himself and the reader some variety. Whatever one may think of the cosmic scheme of 23 ff., Plato clearly feels it is a discovery of some importance; and scientific method was and is an important topic.

PHILEBUS

The numbers and letters that appear in the margin are the standard means of precise reference to Plato. They refer to the pages and sections of pages of the edition of Plato by Stephanus, Geneva, 1578.

An asterisk in the margin indicates that there is a note in the Textual Appendix, pp. 151–2.

CHARACTERS OF THE DIALOGUE:
SOCRATES, PROTARCHUS, PHILEBUS

SOCRATES: So, Protarchus, consider the thesis you are 11a
poised to take over from Philebus, and the one advanced by me
against which you are about to argue – that is, if you don't b
agree with it. Would you like me to summarize them?

PROTARCHUS: Yes, please.

SOCRATES: Well, Philebus says that for all living creatures the good is enjoyment, pleasure, delight and whatever is
compatible with them. But my contention is that they are not
the good, but that reason, intellect, memory – not to mention
their cognates, correct belief and true calculation – are far better than pleasure for all creatures capable of attaining them;[1] c
they offer the greatest benefit for all those who, now or in the
future, are able to attain them. Isn't this, Philebus, more or
less what each of us is saying?[2]

PHILEBUS: Absolutely, Socrates.

SOCRATES: So, Protarchus, this is the thesis which is now
being offered to you – do you accept it?

PROTARCHUS: I have to, since our fine friend Philebus
has backed down.

---

1. Notice that Socrates does not commit himself to saying that his candidates are *the* good, just that they are better than pleasure. Shortly he will mention the possibility of there being 'some other condition' which is better than
both pleasure and reason: then see 20b ff. where it is proved that neither is *the*
good.

2. The same dichotomy between pleasure and reason as candidates for the
summum bonum is mentioned at *Republic* 505b and is resolved at 576b–588a
with a recommendation of the life of the philosopher, similar in many respects
to the life to be recommended in the *Philebus*.

SOCRATES: We must make every effort to determine the truth of these matters, mustn't we?

d PROTARCHUS: Yes, we must.

SOCRATES: Now, there's something else for us to agree on.

PROTARCHUS: What?

SOCRATES: That each of us will now try to show which state or condition of the soul is able to fulfil every man's life.[1] Isn't that what we will do?

PROTARCHUS: Yes.

SOCRATES: And pleasure is your candidate, reason mine?

PROTARCHUS: Right.

SOCRATES: What if we find a better state? If it turns out

e to be more akin to pleasure, wouldn't it follow that the life of pleasure would beat the life of reason, but *both* would be

12*a* defeated by the life whose property this state securely is?

PROTARCHUS: Yes.

SOCRATES: Alternatively, if it turns out to be more akin to reason, then reason beats pleasure, and pleasure is the loser. What do you think? Shall we take these points as settled?

PROTARCHUS: *I* think we should.

SOCRATES: What about you, Philebus? What do you think?

PHILEBUS: I think and will continue to think that pleasure is the winner on every count. But you, Protarchus, must find out for yourself.

PROTARCHUS: Since you have handed the argument over to me, Philebus, you should no longer take it upon yourself to agree or disagree with Socrates.

b PHILEBUS: You're right. I do in fact release myself from

---

1. Notice the restriction to man's life, which was also implicit in the pre-liminary sketch of Socrates' position in 11b–c: this sets the tone of the dia-logue as (i) an attack on Philebus' hedonism which includes all creatures in its purview (11b, cf. 67b); (ii) an ethical treatise, not a metaphysical one, that is, not an examination of the Form of the Good as in the central books of the *Republic*.

my obligation, and I now invoke the goddess herself[1] to witness this.

PROTARCHUS: We too can bear witness for you, that your position is as you say. Well now, Socrates, whether Philebus is agreeable or not, let's try all the same to proceed in due order with the issues that arise.

SOCRATES: Yes, we must try; and we must begin with this goddess, who according to Philebus is called Aphrodite, but whose truest name is Pleasure.

PROTARCHUS: Right.

SOCRATES: When faced with the names of deities, Protarchus, my fear knows no bounds: I always get more afraid than you would think humanly possible. So now I address Aphrodite by whatever title is pleasing to her[2]; but I know that Pleasure is many-faceted, so if we are to begin with her as I suggested, we must be careful in our investigation of her nature. You see, to judge by the singleness of the word, she is single; but nevertheless she assumes all kinds of guises, which are in a sense dissimilar to one another.[3] Consider the following: we talk of the pleasure that the man with no self-control finds, but also of the pleasure the self-controlled man finds in self-control;[4] and again, we talk of the pleasure the stupid man finds, who is full of foolish beliefs and hopes,[5] but also of the

c

d

---

1. Aphrodite, the goddess of pleasurable pursuits, and hence Philebus' personal deity.

2. The Greek deities had many titles, and this, coupled with the belief in the magical power of the correct name, resulted in the tendency to use in prayer some blanket form of address such as this. See also 30d, 61c, 63b; *Cratylus* 400d–e gives Plato's rationale of such forms of address. In effect what Socrates is saying here in the contrast between Aphrodite and Pleasure is that Aphrodite is divine whatever her guise, but Pleasure may not be.

3. In the Greek myths the gods often visit men in various disguises; e.g. Athene in Homer, *Odyssey* I, 96 ff.

4. See *Gorgias* 493d ff. for a vivid expression of the difference between these two sorts of pleasure.

5. See 39e–40b.

pleasure the rational man finds in reason. If anyone claimed in either case that one of these pleasures was similar to the other, wouldn't he be thought a fool, and rightly so?

PROTARCHUS: It's true that these pleasures are found in opposite situations, Socrates, but they are not themselves opposed to one another. How could they be? Isn't pleasure the most similar thing of all to pleasure, as being itself in relation to itself?[1]

SOCRATES: My dear fellow, yes, as colour is to colour. In the respect that all colour is colour there will be no difference; but take black in relation to white: we all recognize that black is not just different from white, but is the exact opposite. Furthermore, shape stands to shape in the same way: generically, all shape is one; but some of its parts are exactly opposed to one another, and others have enormous diversity. There are plenty of other examples of the same phenomenon to be found. So don't rely on this argument of yours that identifies all contraries. I suspect we shall find that some pleasures are opposed to others.

PROTARCHUS: Maybe; but how will this affect my thesis?

SOCRATES: Because we shall claim that, given their dissimilarity, to call all pleasant things good, as you do, is inappropriate. Now, the *pleasantness* of pleasures is not in dispute; but whereas we assert that the majority of pleasures are bad, though some are good,[2] you are attributing goodness to all of them, though you would admit, if pressed, that they are dissimilar. So the question is, what is the common feature of bad and good pleasures alike, thanks to which you are attributing goodness to all of them?

PROTARCHUS: What are you saying, Socrates? I mean, do you imagine that someone whose starting-point is that pleasure is the good will agree to that, and so let you get away with

---

* An asterisk in the margin signifies that there is a note in the Textual Appendix, pp. 151–2.

1. cf. *Gorgias* 494e–495a.

2. cf. *Gorgias* 506c–509c, *Republic* 576c–588a, *Hippias Major* 297e–304a and *Philebus* 31b–55c.

saying that although some pleasures are good, others are bad?   *c*

SOCRATES: But you will admit that they are dissimilar and that some are opposite to one another.

PROTARCHUS: Not in so far as they are pleasures.

SOCRATES: That's a regressive move, Protarchus, which will make us adopt the same old position of denying differences between pleasures and claiming that they are all alike. If we miss the point of my recent examples, we're liable to behave and speak like people whom inexperience makes completely incapable of holding a discussion.   *d*

PROTARCHUS: What do you mean?

SOCRATES: Well, let me mirror your defence. Suppose I stubbornly maintain that what is most dissimilar is most similar of all to that to which it is most dissimilar.[1] Then I'll be able to say the same things you've been saying, our disgraceful incompetence will be revealed and our discussion will be 'shipwrecked and lost'[2]. So let's manoeuvre the discussion back again. If we meet fair and square, it may be possible for us to reach a measure of agreement.

PROTARCHUS: How?   *e*

SOCRATES: Suppose that I'm again being questioned by you, Protarchus.

PROTARCHUS: On what?

SOCRATES: Take reason, knowledge, intellect and everything that I submitted at the beginning as being good when I was asked what the good is: won't they suffer the same fate as your candidates?

PROTARCHUS: What?

SOCRATES: We will find that the sum total of branches of knowledge is more than one, and that some of them are

1. That is, simply because 'dissimilar' is verbally the same as 'dissimilar', as 'pleasure' is to 'pleasure' (see 12d–e): Protarchus has ignored Socrates' warning of 12c–d, as Socrates will point out in 15d–e.

2. The Greek scans: it could be a fragmentary quotation from a lost play, or a snatch of verse composed by Plato himself. The naval metaphor is continued in the next sentence and is particularly appropriate here since the word for 'shipwreck' can also mean 'digress'.

dissimilar to one another; some of them may actually turn out
14a to be opposed in some way, but would I deserve to join in this
discussion if I were worried by this fact into denying that any
of them can be dissimilar to any other? If I did that, then 'here
endeth' our discussion, and we would 'live happily ever after'
thanks only to an absurdity.[1]

PROTARCHUS: I agree: we must avoid that — apart from
living happily ever after! Instead I approve of the parity of your
position with mine: we'll take it that there are many pleasures,
even dissimilar ones, and many different branches of knowledge too.

b SOCRATES: Well, Protarchus, now that we're not conceal-
* ing the diversity within my good and within yours, but are
bringing it out into the open, let's persevere to see if, when
* our candidates are being examined,[2] they may somehow reveal
whether pleasure or reason or some other third thing must be
declared to be the good. I mention the possibility of some
third thing because I assume that we're not just involved in a
contest for the victory of one of our sets of candidates; no, we
must both champion the absolute truth.

PROTARCHUS: Indeed we must.

c SOCRATES: Well, there's another issue which needs our
endorsement even more.

PROTARCHUS: What?

SOCRATES: Everyone finds this issue problematic, though
while some occasionally welcome the difficulty, others don't.

1. The Greek is literally 'our discussion would "end" just like a story, and
we would be "safe" thanks only to an absurdity.' The references are to two
ways in which Greek stories concluded when told to children: 'the story is
ended' and 'the story is safe (i.e. complete)'. The translation is intended to
capture similar connotations for the English reader.

2. There is a strong vein of forensic imagery throughout the dialogue, as if
reason and pleasure were on trial. This recurs most often in the idea that a
verdict or decision about pleasure and reason must be reached (20e, 27c, 33a,
41b, 44d, 50e, 52e, 55c, 58a, 59d, 64d, 65a, b, 66c, 67a, b), but also in the
idea of cross-examination (14b, 23a, 52d, 55c), of giving evidence (47d, 59b,
66d, 67b), of charges (22c) and, even when somewhat inappropriate, of
acquittal (67a).

PROTARCHUS: Please explain more clearly.

SOCRATES: I mean the one which has just dropped into our laps, which by its very nature causes perplexity. You see, the assertion that the many are one and that the one is many is certainly perplexing, and it's easy to argue against anyone who takes either position.

PROTARCHUS: Surely you don't mean the claim that I, Protarchus, am one by nature, but am also many Protarchuses, *d* which are even opposed to one another? Is this the position you mean, that the same person is big and small, heavy and light, and so on and so forth?[1]

SOCRATES: No, Protarchus. The puzzles about the one and the many that you mention have gained wide circulation, but by now almost everyone has agreed to ignore such puzzles on principle, because they take them to be childish, simplistic and highly obstructive to discussion. They make this assumption because[2] they also agree to ignore the puzzle of when someone theoretically divides the constituent parts of some ob- *e* ject, and concedes that all of them are that single object and then, laughing scornfully, proves that he has been forced to make the 'monstrous' assertion both that the one is many and infinitely so, and that the many are only one.

PROTARCHUS: What puzzles *do* you mean, then, Socrates, which have been published on this same topic, but have not yet had a pact made about them?

SOCRATES: This is what I mean, my young friend. You *15a* see, when the proposed unit is such that it is a member of the class of things which are generated and perish – as is the sort of unit we were just talking about – then it is taken for granted, as we were just saying, that it need not be seriously scrutinized. However, when the proposed unit is not of this sort, but when the suggestion is that *man, ox, beauty* and *goodness* are

1. A is big in relation to B, small in relation to C, etc. Cf. *Phaedo* 96d–103a.

2. Socrates seems to suggest that the first type of one-and-many problems has been ignored because of a confusion of it with the second, simpler type.

each one, then these units and others like them are subjected to plenty of enthusiastic argument and division.

PROTARCHUS: How?

b   SOCRATES: In the first place, the question arises whether such units should be supposed truly to exist. Second, how these units, each of which is always the same and admits neither generation nor destruction, should be supposed to be reliably the unit that each is, despite also being present in the infinite number of things which *are* generated – the same unit, you see, is simultaneously in the one and in the many. Should one suppose that this occurs through its being divided up and having become many, or through the whole of it being separated from itself – which seems absolutely impossible?[1] *These*

c   puzzles about *this* sort of one and many, Protarchus, not the others, are responsible for total confusion if they are not properly resolved, and for the removal of difficulties if they are.[2]

PROTARCHUS: So, Socrates, shouldn't this be our immediate project?

SOCRATES: In *my* opinion, yes.

PROTARCHUS: Well, you can assume that the rest of us agree with you on this; as for Philebus, it's probably best not to consult him at the moment, but to let sleeping dogs lie.[3]

d   SOCRATES: Quite so. Now, since there is considerable wrangling of all sorts in this controversy, the question is where to start. Why not from here?

PROTARCHUS: From where?

SOCRATES: It's not too hard to see – it's not a new phenomenon – that unity and plurality crop up in every single

---

1. Does each good thing, say, possess a portion of goodness, or the whole of goodness? The latter possibility is immediately rejected, presumably on the grounds that it involves there being as many 'wholes' as there are good things, in addition to the original whole which is goodness itself. See *Parmenides* 131a ff.

2. For another statement of Plato's estimation of the philosophical importance of this one-and-many problem, see *Laws* 965b ff.

3. The Greek proverb is: 'Don't move something bad when it's fine where it is.'

utterance, but that speech identifies them in the process.[1] This will never stop being the case, nor has it just begun: such a phenomenon is, in my opinion, an 'immortal and ageless'[2] feature of human speech itself. As soon as a young man gets wind of it, he is delighted: he feels he has discovered a treasure-trove of ingenuity. He is in his seventh heaven, and he loves to wor- *e* ry every sentence, now shaking it to and fro and lumping it together, now rolling it out again and tearing it apart.[3] Above all he confuses himself, but he also confuses anyone he ever comes across, be he younger, older or of the same age as himself. He spares neither his father nor his mother, nor anything which can hear – even animals barely escape, let alone men: he *16a* wouldn't have mercy on a foreigner, if he could only get hold of an interpreter!

PROTARCHUS: Socrates, don't you see how many of us there are, and that we are all young? Doesn't this make you afraid that if you insult us, we might join forces with Philebus and set about *you*? All the same, we know what you mean; so if there are any ways or means of avoiding such chaos in our discussion without provoking bad feeling, and of finding some better method than this for approaching the subject, then *b* please don't hesitate to avail yourself of it, and we will follow as best we can. I hope we keep up – this is quite a lengthy argument we've let ourselves in for, Socrates.

SOCRATES: It is indeed, my boys, as Philebus calls you. Still, there neither is nor could there be any better method than the one of which I have always been enamoured, but which has often eluded me and left me all alone and confused.

PROTARCHUS: Let's hear what it is.

1. To say '*x* is F' seems to be to identify *x* and F-ness, if the 'is' of identity ('a tome is a volume') is confused with the 'is' of predication ('the sky is blue').

2. A Homeric description of the gods.

3. This canine image is also applied to sophistry at *Sophist* 259c and *Republic* 539b, where it is again used of the almost unwitting confusion of young men. For the specific confusion referred to here, see also *Sophist* 251b–c and *Politicus* 285a–b.

c   SOCRATES: It is not very difficult to explain, but it is exceedingly difficult to apply: anything which is a suitable object of science and has ever been discovered has been brought to light by this process. See for yourself what process I mean.

PROTARCHUS: Tell me then.

SOCRATES: It seems to me that it was a gift of the gods to mankind, hurled from heaven along with the brightest of fire, thanks to some Prometheus.[1] Men of old, being superior to us and dwelling nearer the gods, transmitted this saying: while the things that are ever said to exist consist of one and many, yet they also innately have within themselves limit and indeterminacy.[2] It follows, since they are composed in this

d   way, that we must always assume a single concept in every case, and look for it: we will find it since it is present.[3] So, if we grasp it, we must see if there are two in the next stage, or three, if there are not two, or some other number.[4] Moreover, we must treat each of *these* units in the same way, until we see not only that the original unit is one and many and an indeterminate number, but also *how* many it is. Only when the whole

e   number between the indeterminate and the single unit has been grasped can the concept of indeterminacy be applied to the plurality: then and only then can each of all the units be dismissed and released into the indeterminate. The gods, as I

1. Prometheus was a mythological benefactor of mankind: he gave fire to man when Zeus had withheld it, and taught man all the basic sciences. Hence he is a suitable figurehead here, as this tradition is an analysis of what it is in anything which enables it to be an object of science. Pythagoras is probably meant by 'some Prometheus', since the notion of limit and indeterminacy is peculiarly Pythagorean (see Aristotle, *Metaphysics* 986a 15–21), as is the study of music (985b 23 ff.) and of letters (1093a 20 ff.), which are used by Plato as examples in what follows.

2. This will be explained in what follows; on limit (*peras*) and indeterminacy (*apeiron*) see further Introduction p. 40 ff. It has not been possible to translate *apeiron* identically throughout, though there are only three deviations from the standard 'indeterminate': 'infinite' (14e, 15b) and 'boundless' (17e – this to capture a Platonic pun).

3. cf. *Politicus* 285a–b.

4. cf. *Politicus* 287c.

said, taught us by this tradition how to investigate, learn and teach one another; but contemporary wiseacres come up with a 17a unit and plurality too quickly or too slowly;[1] there's no *system* to their procedure. Then they make the unit indeterminate straight away, and fail to demarcate the intermediates. I must stress that it's the intermediates that make all the difference between whether our discussion is conducted in a philosophical or merely a contentious manner.[2]

PROTARCHUS: I think I more or less understand some of what you're saying, Socrates, but I could do with a clearer statement of the rest.

SOCRATES: Well, Protarchus, the alphabet which was the basis of your education is a clear example of what I'm talking about, so use it to see what I mean.   b

PROTARCHUS: How?

SOCRATES: As you know, vocal sound as spoken by any one person or by everyone is a single phenomenon, and yet is also quantitatively indeterminate.

PROTARCHUS: Of course.

SOCRATES: And neither the knowledge that it is indeterminate nor that it is single makes any of us experts: literacy comes from knowing the number and nature of its parts.

PROTARCHUS: Very true.

SOCRATES: Moreover, musical knowledge too is acquired in the same way.

PROTARCHUS: How?

SOCRATES: In the domain of this science too vocal sound c is single, as you know.

PROTARCHUS: Of course.

SOCRATES: But don't you think we should postulate the dichotomy of low and high pitch? And thirdly even pitch?

PROTARCHUS: Yes.

SOCRATES: But if that's all you know, you still won't be a

1. Either they omit subdivisions or they subdivide too much. Cf. *Politicus* 262b, 264b, 277a–b.

2. cf. *Republic* 454a, *Politicus* 262b.

musical expert, though if you're ignorant of them you'll be almost completely useless in the subject.

PROTARCHUS: Quite.

SOCRATES: But, my friend, when you know how many intervals there are in height and depth of sound, when you
d know their nature and the boundaries of the intervals and the systems that they form,[1] which our predecessors, who discovered them, have taught us, their successors, to call 'scales' — they also discovered other similar features in bodily movements, and they tell us that these too should be measured numerically and called 'tempos' and 'measures', and, they add, we should realize the necessity of studying *every* unit and plurality from this point of view — anyway, when you understand *these* matters, you're an expert; and by examining and under-
e standing any other unit in this manner, you become knowledgeable about it. On the other hand, the boundless plurality of individual things and in individual things makes you bound for ignorance! You are of no account, you amount to nothing, since you have never looked at the amount of anything!

PROTARCHUS: I think Socrates has expressed himself very well, Philebus.

18a PHILEBUS: I agree. But what on earth is he getting at by bringing these points up now?

SOCRATES: You know, Protarchus, that's a fair question of Philebus'.

PROTARCHUS: Of course it is; answer him, then.

SOCRATES: I will, when I have gone through these matters a little more. Whenever anyone perceives any unit he must, as we said, take some number into consideration and not make straight for the indeterminate. The same goes for the opposite situation, when he is forced to take the indeterminate
b first: again, he must not make a rush for the unit, but he must attend to the number which circumscribes each plurality and eventually reach the unit only when the whole number has

1. 'A *system* must be seen as a compound of one or more intervals' (Aristoxenus, *The Principals and Elements of Harmonics*, I.16).

been seen. Once again, let's use the alphabet to understand what's meant by this.

PROTARCHUS: How?

SOCRATES: Some god, or some man of divine stature – the Egyptians say that it was Theuth[1] – once saw that vocal sound is indeterminate. He was the first to perceive the vowels in that indeterminate and to notice that there are several of them, not just one. He also realized that there are other letters which do not consist of sound as such, but nevertheless do make some *c* noise,[2] and he noted that they too have some number; and he distinguished a third class of letters, which we nowadays call 'mutes'. Next he divided these noiseless, mute letters until he reached each unit;[3] and he divided the vowels and the intermediate letters in the same way until, once he had seen their number, he gave the name 'letter' to each and every unit. Now, since he saw that none of us would understand any of the letters as it is in itself, in isolation from the rest, he further concluded that this interdependence is a factor which unifies *d* all the letters in some way; so he declared that there is a single science for them, which he called 'literacy'.

PHILEBUS: I understand these points about the relations of letters to one another even more clearly than the former example, Protarchus. I still find the argument incomplete, however, in the same way that I did a short while ago.

SOCRATES: No doubt, Philebus, you're again referring to its relevance.

1. Or Thoth, the Egyptian god of learning, etc.

2. This distinction is not equivalent to what we call voiced as opposed to voiceless consonants. The Greeks classified letters according to how much breath is used in sounding them: thus those which use the most breath are the vowels (literally 'the sounded ones'); those which use the least are the mutes (our 'stops'); and between these are what Aristotle was the first to call the semi-vowels, which include various Greek letters we would class as nasals, sibilants and continuants. Cf. *Cratylus* 424c–d and *Theaetetus* 203b for the same division of letters in Plato.

3. So at first he merely noticed that there was more than one member of each class; now he distinguishes each letter of each class.

PHILEBUS: Yes, that's what Protarchus and I have been wanting to know for some time.

SOCRATES: You say you've been wanting to know for some time, but I guarantee that the knowledge is already *e* within your reach.

PHILEBUS: How?

SOCRATES: Our argument has from the start been about whether reason or pleasure is preferable, hasn't it?

PHILEBUS: Of course.

SOCRATES: And we reckon that each of them is single.

PHILEBUS: Indeed we do.

SOCRATES: So the preceding argument requires us to answer these questions: how is each of them both one and *19a** many? How are they not just indeterminate? Rather, what number does each of them have before becoming indeterminately many?

PROTARCHUS: I don't know how, Philebus, but Socrates has somehow led us round in a circle; and it's no simple question he has introduced. Which of us do you think should answer it? I'm probably making a fool of myself in asking you, just because I can't answer the present question, to take over again, when I have fully committed myself to taking your place in the argument. I think it would be far more absurd, *b* however, if neither of us were able to answer. So what do you think we should do? The point of Socrates' question seems to be whether there are varieties of pleasure or not, and how many there are, and their nature; and likewise with regard to reason.

SOCRATES: Son of Callias, you're absolutely right. We would all be completely and utterly worthless as long as we were unable to perform this operation[1] on everything since, as the preceding argument demonstrated, it is a case not just of unity, similarity and identity, but also of opposition.

c PROTARCHUS: I suppose you're right, Socrates. But although it'd be nice for the wise man to know everything, I think the next best thing for him is to have a proper estimation

---

1. To discover how many varieties there are, etc.

of himself.[1] Why am I saying this just now? I'll tell you. You've given all of us the benefit of your company, Socrates, and have committed yourself to help find out what is the best thing man can have. You denied Philebus' assertion that pleasure, delight, enjoyment and so on are the greatest good, and you proposed instead those things which we quite rightly keep *d* reminding ourselves of, so that we have the alternatives juxtaposed in our minds for investigation. Your claim, it seems, is that the good which should properly be called better than pleasure is intellect, knowledge, understanding and science, not to mention all their cognates; and that man ought to have these rather than what Philebus suggested. So when both claims had been made – not without argument – we teased you and threatened that we would not let you go home until the issue *e* had been concluded and brought to a satisfactory limit.[2] You agreed and gave yourself to us for this purpose.[3] What we're saying, then, as children might, is that a gift properly given can't be taken back: so you must change your attitude towards the present discussion and stop treating us like this.

SOCRATES: Like what?

PROTARCHUS: You keep getting us into difficulties and *20a* asking us things we couldn't answer satisfactorily at the moment. I hope we are not to suppose that the goal of this conversation is to get us all into difficulties.[4] No; if we are unable to do the job, then it's up to you: that was your promise. That is why you yourself must decide whether you need to distin-

1. i.e. Protarchus does not know everything, but he has enough *sophrosyne* to be aware of his limitations: so he calls on Socrates to answer the question himself. The Greek virtue of *sophrosyne* comprised both self-knowledge and self-control.

2. Protarchus' use of 'limit' is rather strained: it is meant to be a pun (cf. 16c ff.)

3. All this, of course, does not occur within our dialogue, but adds colour. Similar touches occur at 11a–b, 50d–e, 67b.

4. This was explicitly the goal of the early Socratic dialogues, on the principle that knowing that we do not know something is better than thinking that we do.

guish the varieties of pleasure and knowledge, or whether you needn't bother: if there is conceivably an alternative way offering other means of clarifying our present dispute, and if you are able to take it, then please do.

b   SOCRATES: Since you put it like that, you may rest assured that someone like me will give you no further cause for alarm. Whenever you're afraid, say 'please' and fear is banished. Moreover one of the gods seems to have reminded me of something useful.

PROTARCHUS: What do you mean? What have you remembered?

SOCRATES: A theory about pleasure and reason now occurs to me, one which I once heard long ago in a dream, or I might even have been awake;[1] it held that neither of them is the good, but that there is some other third thing, different from them and better than them. One result of finding out for cer-
c tain about this third thing would be the demotion of pleasure, which could no longer be identified with the good. Isn't that so?

PROTARCHUS: Yes.

SOCRATES: Also I don't think we'll have any further need to classify the varieties of pleasure. But time will tell.

PROTARCHUS: That's good to hear. Now bring the discussion to an equally excellent conclusion.

SOCRATES: First there are still some minor points on which we should agree.

PROTARCHUS: What are they?

d   SOCRATES: Consider what the good must inevitably be: should it be perfect or imperfect?

PROTARCHUS: It must of course be the most perfect thing of all, Socrates.

---

1. Socrates also 'recalls' a theory in a similar way (in *déjà vu*, as it were) at *Cratylus* 439c and *Theaetetus* 201d. The only common philosophical denominator seems to be that the 'dreamed' theory seems to Plato to have greater *prima facie* plausibility than the theories which precede it in each dialogue. But if when tested it turns out to be false, it is said to be only a dream after all (*Theaetetus* 208b).

SOCRATES: And isn't the good bound to be sufficient?[1]

PROTARCHUS: Yes, indeed; it must surpass everything in this respect too.

SOCRATES: There's one thing in particular, however, which I think must be said about it: that all creatures which recognize it want to gain it and possess it for their very own; so they track it down and aim for it, with no concern for anything which is not ultimately accompanied by goodness.

PROTARCHUS: That is undeniable.

SOCRATES: Then let's investigate the life of pleasure and *e* that of reason, and reach a verdict about them by looking at them separately.[2]

PROTARCHUS: What do you mean?

SOCRATES: I mean by banning reason from the life of pleasure and pleasure from the life of reason. You see, if either of them is the good, it must lack nothing at all; and if either of them is shown to be lacking, then, as I'm sure you realize, 21a it can no longer be said to be our true good.

PROTARCHUS: Of course not.

SOCRATES: Shall we use you as the subject of our experimental test of them?

PROTARCHUS: By all means.

SOCRATES: Answer me this, then.

PROTARCHUS: What?

SOCRATES: Would *you*, Protarchus, gladly live your whole life experiencing the greatest pleasures?

PROTARCHUS: Why not?

SOCRATES: So, suppose you have such a life, to the fullest extent: would you think you were still lacking anything?

1. Perfection seems to imply self-sufficiency; sufficiency implies that it will be enough for any creature that attains it.

2. Plato clearly does not believe that in real life they can be separated like this. The separation is artificial, designed to reduce to absurdity the view that either of them is the good, but particularly Philebus' view that pleasure is the *sole* good (11b): for it follows from his claim, as distinct from Socrates' more guarded claim about this candidates, that pleasure ought to be good even apart from any of Socrates' candidates.

PROTARCHUS: Not at all.

SOCRATES: Now consider carefully: wouldn't there be any
b lack at all of reason, intellect, calculation of what you need and
things of this sort?

PROTARCHUS: Why ever should there be? If I had pleasure, I would, presumably, have all I needed.

SOCRATES: So, with this mode of existence you would
continually be feeling the greatest pleasures throughout your
life, wouldn't you?

PROTARCHUS: Of course.

SOCRATES: But you've got no intellect, memory, knowledge and true judgement; surely it follows, in the first place,
that since you lack reason you can't possibly recognize whether
or not you are feeling pleasure?

PROTARCHUS: Inevitably.

c SOCRATES: Moreover, it is equally inevitable, of course,
that since you've got no memory, you can't remember ever
having felt pleasure, and no memory whatsoever remains of the
pleasure that occurs at any moment. Again, having no true belief, you can't believe that you are feeling pleasure when in fact
you are; and since you lack the ability to calculate, you can't
even calculate how you will feel pleasure in the future. Your
life is not the life of a human being, but of a jellyfish or some
sea creature which is merely a body endowed with life, a com-
d ∗ panion of oysters. Isn't this the situation? How else can we
conceive it?

PROTARCHUS: No other way.

SOCRATES: Is this sort of life worth choosing?

PROTARCHUS: I have absolutely nothing to say at the
moment, Socrates: the argument has overwhelmed me.

SOCRATES: Well, we mustn't give up yet. Next it is the
turn of the life of intellect. We must see . . .

PROTARCHUS: But what sort of life do you mean by this?

SOCRATES: . . . whether anyone would welcome a life in
which he possessed reason, intellect, knowledge and total re-
e call, but experienced not the slightest trace of pleasure, nor of

68

pain either, but was in fact entirely insensible of all such feelings.

PROTARCHUS: *I* wouldn't consider choosing either life, Socrates, and I doubt anyone else ever would either.

SOCRATES: What about the composite life, Protarchus, a 22*a* mixture of both together?[1]

PROTARCHUS: You mean incorporating both pleasure and intellect and reason?

SOCRATES: Yes, and others like them.

PROTARCHUS: This life will certainly be chosen by everyone — everyone without exception — in preference to either of the others.

SOCRATES: I wonder if we realize what conclusion this argument entails?

PROTARCHUS: Yes, of course: that three lives have been proposed, and that neither of the first two is sufficient or desir- *b* able for man or beast.

SOCRATES: So isn't it clear by now that neither of them comprises the good? I mean, if it did, it would have been sufficient and perfect, and every plant[2] and creature which had the ability to do so would have chosen to live its whole life in this condition. If anyone were to choose otherwise, it would not be his fault: it would be ignorance or some unfortunate compulsion that caused him to act contrary to the nature of what is truly desirable.

PROTARCHUS: I suppose you're right.

SOCRATES: Well, I think it has been satisfactorily shown *c* that Philebus' goddess, at least, must not be identified with the good.

1. It seems to be implied that not only the good life, but any human life at all is such a mixture: only lower (21c) or higher (32e ff.) life-forms can live an unmixed life.

2. The inclusion of plants is intended figuratively: at *Timaeus* 77a–c Plato claims that a plant is an animal fixed to the ground, and has a soul of a sort; nevertheless it remains true that even on this view a plant does not have the ability to live such a life!

PHILEBUS: Yes, but neither is your intellect the good, Socrates: presumably it is liable to the same charges.

SOCRATES: Perhaps that's true for *my* intellect, Philebus; but I don't think we've touched on anything relevant to the true and divine intellect. Anyway, although I won't champion intellect against the integrated life for the first prize, we must still consider our courses of action where the second prize is concerned. You see, it's conceivable that each of us might claim that his own candidate is responsible for the integrated life, the one saying that intellect is responsible, the other pleasure. If this happened, then while neither of them would be the good, responsibility might possibly be assigned to one or the other.[1] As far as *this* is concerned, however, Philebus would meet with even stronger opposition from me: the mixed life is desirable and good through its possession of something, and I would contend that intellect, not pleasure, is more akin and more similar to that something, whatever it is.[2] If I was right, it would be false to say that pleasure is entitled to the first or even the second prize. In fact, if my intellect is at all to be trusted at the moment, pleasure doesn't even get the third prize.[3]

PROTARCHUS: Well, Socrates, *I* am now inclined to think that pleasure has been knocked to the ground, as it were, by your arguments: in the fight for first prize, it is out for the count. And I think it ought to be said that it was with good reason that intellect didn't try for the first prize – it would only have suffered the same fate. But if pleasure were deprived of the *second* prize, it would be altogether dishonoured in the eyes of its admirers: it would no longer seem so attractive, even to them.

SOCRATES: What are we to do, then? Is the better course

1. Responsibility for the goodness of the mixture, not for the mixing of the ingredients, as what immediately follows shows.

2. See 64c–66a.

3. See 66a–c.

to let pleasure stand down immediately and not to cause it pain by the most searching tests and examinations?

PROTARCHUS: You're talking nonsense, Socrates.

SOCRATES: Is that because what I said is impossible, 'to *b* cause pleasure pain'?

PROTARCHUS: Not just that. I meant that you are also failing to appreciate that none of us is going to let you go yet, not until you have concluded the discussion.

SOCRATES: So be it, then, Protarchus. But what a long argument there is ahead of us, and one which, as things stand, is not going to be very easy. In fact I think that new tactics are called for: if I am to champion intellect for the second prize, I must arm myself, so to speak, with different weapons from those I used before, though there may be some overlap. Don't you think that's what I should do?

PROTARCHUS: Of course.

SOCRATES: We must be sure to pay special attention to *c* establishing the starting-point.

PROTARCHUS: What do you have in mind?

SOCRATES: Let's divide everything that now exists in the universe into two, or rather, if you have no objection, into three classes.

PROTARCHUS: On what principle? Please explain.

SOCRATES: Let's take some of our recent points.

PROTARCHUS: Which ones?

SOCRATES: We said that god revealed both indeterminacy and limit in things, didn't we?

PROTARCHUS: Certainly.

SOCRATES: Then let's assume that these are two of the classes, and that the third is a unit formed by the mixture of *d* them both. I'm afraid you might think I'm being flippant and silly in this division and enumeration of classes.   *

PROTARCHUS: My dear fellow, what makes you say that?

SOCRATES: Because I think I need yet another class, a fourth one.

PROTARCHUS: Tell me what it is.

SOCRATES: I want you to count the cause of the mixing of the first two classes with each other as a fourth class over and above the other three.

PROTARCHUS: So won't you also need a fifth, to effect dissolution?

SOCRATES: Perhaps. I don't think I need a fifth at the moment, but if I ever do, I hope you'll excuse me if I pursue it.[1]

PROTARCHUS: Of course.

SOCRATES: First let's keep three of the four separate, and let's try to ascertain how two of them are each a unit and a plurality. We can do this by considering each of them when they are divided and fragmented into many parts and by then reassembling them into their respective units.

PROTARCHUS: Perhaps you could explain them to me even more clearly; then I'd probably understand.

24a SOCRATES: Well, I'm talking about the two which, I suggest, are the same as just now; the indeterminate and the determinant. Let's leave the determinant for a while, but I'll try now to show how the indeterminate is a plurality.

PROTARCHUS: All right.

SOCRATES: Now pay careful attention. Don't be put off even though what I'm asking you to consider is complex and problematical. Take 'hotter' and 'colder': in the first place see whether you find any *limit* in them or whether, since 'more and less' dwells in them, as long as it does, it cannot allow completion. For the occurrence of an end would be the end of it!

PROTARCHUS: Yes, you're quite right.

* SOCRATES: In other words, 'hotter' and 'colder' are always imbued with 'more and less'.

PROTARCHUS: Very much so.

SOCRATES: So the implication of the argument is that they never have an end. And, of course, if they are endless, they are absolutely indeterminate.

PROTARCHUS: Rather, Socrates.

---

1. Nothing is made of this possibility. Perhaps it should be put down to humour in the sense that it picks up Socrates' (ironic) fear of appearing silly.

SOCRATES: My dear Protarchus, how well you have understood the point! Thank you for reminding me that this 'rather' you have just mentioned,[1] and 'hardly' too, have the c same effect as 'more and less': wherever they are present they prevent the existence of any definite quantity. Instead, by imbuing each state of affairs with 'rather more than hardly at all', or vice versa, they give rise to 'to a greater and lesser degree' and they eradicate 'just this quantity'. You see, as I said a short while ago, if they don't eradicate definite quantity, if 'more and less' and 'rather and hardly' don't prevent definite quantity d and moderation[2] from entering their stronghold, then they will be displaced from the position they occupied. For if 'hotter' and 'colder' were to admit definite quantity, they would cease to exist. I mean, 'hotter' is perpetually increasing and never stays still, and the same goes for 'colder'; but anything with definite quantity is stable and has stopped increasing. So according to this account 'hotter' would be indeterminate, and so would its opposite.

PROTARCHUS: Well, yes, it does look that way, Socrates, though as you said, these matters are not easy to understand. Perhaps if we discussed it over and over again, we would find that there is, in fact, enough agreement between us. e

SOCRATES: Well said! That's what we must try to achieve. But for the moment – to avoid a complete exposition, which would take us a long time – see whether we can accept the following as the mark of indeterminacy.

PROTARCHUS: What mark do you mean?

SOCRATES: Everything which we find becoming more and less, and admitting 'rather and hardly' and 'excessively' and so on, we must classify as indeterminates, and take this to be a $25a$ single class. This procedure is in accordance with what we said before: as you probably remember, we said that we must do

1. Socrates jokingly prefers to understand Protarchus' 'rather' as explaining indeterminacy rather than the extent of his agreement.

2. Moderation might seem out of place here, but it is a feature of Greek comparatives that they can mean not just 'more x' but also 'too x'.

our best to assemble fragments and segments and to recognize the mark of a single nature.

PROTARCHUS: I remember.

SOCRATES: So the things which do *not* admit these properties, but admit all their opposites – 'equal' and equality, in the first place, and besides 'equal', 'double' and

b everything which is a numerical or metrical relation – all these we would be right to assign to limit.[1] What do you think?

PROTARCHUS: Absolutely right, Socrates.

SOCRATES: So far, so good. But now for the third class, the one which is a mixture of both of these: what character shall we say it has?

PROTARCHUS: It is *you* that will have to tell *me*, I think.

SOCRATES: No, it will have to be a god, provided one of them listens to my prayers.

PROTARCHUS: Pray, then, and see.

SOCRATES: All right. Well, one of them *does* seem to be befriending us now, Protarchus.

c PROTARCHUS: What makes you think so?

SOCRATES: Don't worry, I'll tell you. You concentrate on what I say.

PROTARCHUS: Go on.

SOCRATES: We were talking briefly just now of 'hotter' and 'colder', weren't we?

PROTARCHUS: Yes.

SOCRATES: Add to them 'dryer' and 'wetter', 'greater' and 'fewer', 'faster' and 'slower', 'larger' and 'smaller', and all the things we previously assigned to a unit consisting of whatever admits 'more and less'.

d PROTARCHUS: Do you mean the indeterminate?

SOCRATES: Yes. Now, the next step is to mix in with it the class of limit.

PROTARCHUS: Which class is that?

1. The sentence is ambiguous: it is not clear whether equality, etc., are being said to be the things which admit the opposites of 'more and less' and so on, or whether they are themselves the opposite properties which some things admit. Section 25d resolves the ambiguity: they are the opposite properties.

SOCRATES: The one we should have assembled just now. Just as we assembled the class of indeterminacy into a unit, so we should have assembled the class of limitation too, but didn't.[1] It'll probably make no difference, however, as long as we get clear on it now when both these classes are combined.

PROTARCHUS: What *is* its nature? What do you mean?

SOCRATES: I mean the class of 'equal' and 'double' and whatever stops opposites being at odds with one another, and makes them proportionate and harmonious by implanting *e* number.

PROTARCHUS: I see. You seem to me to be saying that the inclusion of these factors in the mixture results in each case in the production of things.

SOCRATES: That's right.

PROTARCHUS: Go on, then.

SOCRATES: Isn't health the result of the proper integration of these factors in cases of sickness?[2]

PROTARCHUS: Unquestionably.

26a

SOCRATES: And doesn't their proper integration in height and depth and speed and slowness, which are indeterminates, have the same result? That is, it creates limit, and forms the entire foundation of the whole art of music.

PROTARCHUS: Admirably put.

SOCRATES: Furthermore, when it occurs in wintry storms or stifling heat, it removes gross excess and indeterminacy, and creates due measure and proportion.

PROTARCHUS: Certainly.

SOCRATES: So from the mixing of indeterminates and *b*

1. This resolves the ambiguity mentioned on p. 74. The class of limitation has not been assembled because, although we have been given equality, etc., as the counterparts of 'more and less', etc., we have not been given the counterparts of 'hotter' and 'colder', etc.

2. In contemporary medicine, a typical belief about health was that it was the proper harmony of the physical elements, which were invariably seen as opposites (e.g. hot and cold). So Plato is saying here that health is the result of these elements being in proportionate relationship with one another, i.e. when they have received limitation.

determinants come climatic conditions[1] and all fine things, don't they?

PROTARCHUS: Of course.

SOCRATES: There are thousands of other cases I could mention, such as beauty, if it is accompanied by health, and physical strength; and the soul too has very many qualities of outstanding beauty.[2] With your good looks, Philebus, you should have known that the goddess herself noticed that imbalance and worthlessness always accommodate limitless pleasures and indulgences, so she established law and order as determinants.[3] Ironically, on your view she was an oppressor;

c but I maintain the opposite, that she was a saviour. What about you, Protarchus? What do you think?

PROTARCHUS: *I* thoroughly approve of what you say.

SOCRATES: So much for those three classes, then, if you understand them.

PROTARCHUS: Well, I think I do. I take you to be saying that the indeterminate is a unit and that another unit, the second, in fact, is the limit in things. But I haven't quite got a firm grasp on what you mean the third one to be.

SOCRATES: That's because the profusion of the third class has disconcerted you, my dear fellow. The indeterminate too, however, certainly engendered a plurality of types, but still

d turned out to be single, since these types were stamped with the seal of 'more' and its opposite.

PROTARCHUS: True.

SOCRATES: Moreover, when we found that limit con-

---

1. Neither heat nor cold is allowed to increase too far or for too long. Alternatively the word translated 'climatic conditions' could be translated 'seasons', in which case Plato has a broader perspective: neither the hot season nor the cold season is allowed to increase too far or to go on for too long, but each is replaced by the other. For this broader perspective, see 28c ff., especially 30b–c.

2. I translate literally 'beauty', though the Greek word (*kalos*) also covers a vast range of commendable properties, to preserve the connection with Aphrodite. See also the relation of beauty to goodness at the end of the dialogue.

3. He addresses Philebus because of an implicit criticism: Philebus' identification of pleasure and Aphrodite (12b) is mistaken. As a deity, Aphrodite is on the side of order, but pleasure is not.

tained a plurality, we didn't captiously declare that its nature *
was not single.

PROTARCHUS: No, of course we didn't.

SOCRATES: Of course not. Now, as regards the third class,
what you must take me to be saying is this: I understand this
unit to consist of all the offspring of the former classes, whose
birth is made possible by the measures which are produced
together with limit.

PROTARCHUS: I see.

SOCRATES: There aren't just three classes, however: we've e
already said that there's a fourth which must be examined.
And we must share the examination: you must decide
whether, in your opinion, there must necessarily be some *cause*
of the generation of anything. [1]

PROTARCHUS: Yes, I think so. How else could it be
generated?

SOCRATES: Isn't it the case that the maker and the cause
differ only in name, not in nature? Wouldn't it be correct to
say that they are identical?

PROTARCHUS: It would.

SOCRATES: Furthermore, we will find that the same 27*a*
obtains also for that which is made and that which is generated. Don't you think that they too differ only in name?

PROTARCHUS: Yes.

SOCRATES: Isn't it a natural law that the maker always
leads and that the product is subsequent in its generation to
the maker?

PROTARCHUS: Yes.

SOCRATES: Therefore the cause is completely different
from that which is dependent on its cause for generation.

PROTARCHUS: Of course.

SOCRATES: Now, weren't our three classes made up from
the things which are generated and the things from which
everything is generated?

PROTARCHUS: Absolutely.

---

1. cf. *Timaeus* 28a, *Hippias Major* 296e ff.

b   SOCRATES: Has what fashions them all been satisfactorily shown to be different from the rest, so that we can pronounce the cause a fourth class?

PROTARCHUS: Yes, it is different.

SOCRATES: Well then, the correct procedure now that the four classes have been distinguished, is to enumerate them in order, so we can be sure to remember each one.

PROTARCHUS: Of course.

SOCRATES: First, then, I am talking about indeterminacy; second, limit; then thirdly something which is a mixture of these and has been generated from them; and would I be wrong if I called the cause of the mixing and of the generation

c   fourth?

PROTARCHUS: Of course not.

SOCRATES: All right, then; what next? What made us want to cover this ground? Wasn't it because we were trying to discover whether the second prize should belong to pleasure or to reason?

PROTARCHUS: Yes, that's it.

SOCRATES: So mightn't it be the case, now that we've made these distinctions, that we are also in a better position to put the finishing touches to the verdict we reached in the original argument about the first and second places?

PROTARCHUS: Probably.

d   SOCRATES: Let's do so, then. I seem to remember that we established the mixed life of both pleasure and reason as the winner, didn't we?

PROTARCHUS: Yes.

SOCRATES: The nature and class of *this* life, at any rate, is surely evident.

PROTARCHUS: Of course.

SOCRATES: In fact, of course, we'll say that it is a part of
* the third class, because our mixed class does not consist of just *some* pairs, but of *all* the indeterminates which have been restrained by limit. Consequently this victorious life must be a part of it.

PROTARCHUS: Perfectly correct.

SOCRATES: So far, so good. But what about *your* life, e
Philebus, which consists of pleasure with no admixture of anything else? In which of the classes we've mentioned would
we be right to put it? Before you reply, first answer another
question.

PHILEBUS: Ask away.

SOCRATES: Are pleasure and pain determinants, or isn't it
rather the case that they are among the things that admit
'more and less'?

PHILEBUS: Yes, Socrates, they admit 'more': pleasure
would not be entirely good if it wasn't so constituted as to be *
indeterminate in both frequency and intensity.

SOCRATES: Nor would pain be entirely bad, Philebus. It 28*a*
follows that something else, but not indeterminacy, is the
relevant cause of the fact that pleasures *are* granted a portion of
goodness.[1] Anyway, as you say, pleasure and pain are among *
the indeterminates;[2] but what about reason, knowledge and
intellect? Tell me, Protarchus, and Philebus too: to which of
the mentioned classes might we assign them without sacrilege? I say 'sacrilege' because I think that a great deal depends
on whether or not we answer this question correctly.

PHILEBUS: That's because you're exaggerating the value of *b*
your god, Socrates.

SOCRATES: And you your goddess, my friend. Be that as
it may, however, we must tackle the question.

PROTARCHUS: Socrates is right, you know, Philebus.
You must do as he says.

PHILEBUS: But didn't you elect to speak on my behalf,
Protarchus?

1. 20b–22b demonstrated that the good life must contain some pleasures;
but 23c–26d demonstrated that no unrestrained indeterminate is good. At
the same time Plato seems to be presupposing the intimate connection between pain and pleasure that he will expound later in the dialogue. Then, if
the indeterminacy of pleasure depends on the indeterminacy of pain, it follows
that its indeterminacy will not guarantee it any goodness, since pain is bad.

2. Aristotle criticizes the view that pleasure is indeterminate at *Nicomachean Ethics* 1173a 15 ff.

PROTARCHUS: Yes, I did, but at the moment I'm in a bit of a quandary. I wish you'd be our seer,[1] Socrates, so that we don't commit the *faux pas* of a discordant statement about your candidate.

c   SOCRATES: Your wish is my command, Protarchus, since the command is easy to obey. But when I was asking to which class intellect and knowledge belong, did my light-hearted valuation, as Philebus put it, really perturb you?

PROTARCHUS: Very much, Socrates.

SOCRATES: Yet the question is simple: all the wise[2] – evaluating themselves in fact[3] – proclaim in unison that intellect is the king of heaven and earth. Presumably they are right. But if you have no objection, let's examine at greater length to which class it belongs.

d   PROTARCHUS: Do as you think best, Socrates. You needn't worry about length for our sake – we won't be annoyed.

SOCRATES: That's good to hear. Well, here's a question that's as good a starting-point as any.

PROTARCHUS: What?

SOCRATES: Are we to say that the universe, this 'whole', as it is called, is controlled by irrationality, randomness and chance? Or are we to say the opposite, as our predecessors did, that it is governed by intellect and the coordination of a wonderful reason?[4]

e   PROTARCHUS: What a question, Socrates! There's a world of difference. I think your first question was quite blas-

---

1. Protarchus continues, both here and in his fear of saying something inappropriate, the notion of the divinity of intellect.

2. Many of the Presocratic philosophers were impressed by the apparent orderliness of the universe; Diogenes of Apollonia and Anaxagoras of Clazomenae, in particular, attributed this to Mind.

3. Because in claiming that intellect governs the universe, they are in effect making a claim about their own intellect, which is a fragment of the whole.

4. See the *Timaeus*, Plato's discussion of the origin and nature of the universe, and *Laws* 886a ff., which are pervaded with Plato's conviction of the orderliness of the universe.

phemous. But to say that intellect regulates the universe does justice to the order we perceive in it, in the sun, moon, stars and the whole vault of heaven. For my part, I can never speak or think about it in any other terms.

SOCRATES: In other words, you want us to join the chorus of our predecessors by agreeing that this is so. You would not 29a have us imagine that we need do no more than repeat others' views without risk to ourselves: no, we too must run the risk of being criticized by some clever fellow who claims that this is *not* how the universe is, but that it is chaotic. Isn't that what you want?

PROTARCHUS: Yes, of course.

SOCRATES: So here's the next point for you to consider.

PROTARCHUS: Go on.

SOCRATES: It concerns the physical make-up of all beings. We can, I think, see that they consist of the following components: fire, water, air — and we can also say, as storm-tossed ✻ sailors do, 'earth ahoy!'[1]

PROTARCHUS: That's a good analogy, because we're b being thoroughly tossed about in this discussion by a storm of difficulties!

SOCRATES: Well now, there's something you must understand about each of these components as they are found in us.

PROTARCHUS: What?

SOCRATES: That each of them, as it is found in us, is trifling in quantity, inferior in quality, thoroughly impure, and hardly deserving of its name.[2] If you recognize this where one of them is concerned, you will be able to see that the same goes for all of them. So take fire as an example: there is fire in us, as you know, and in the universe too.

PROTARCHUS: Of course.

SOCRATES: The fire in us is a trifling thing, feeble and in- c ferior; but the fire in the universe is awesome in quantity and beauty and in all fiery properties.

---

1. See the *Timaeus* for a lengthy discussion of these four elements.

2. cf. Xenophon, *Memorabilia* I. iv. 8.

PROTARCHUS: That is perfectly true.

SOCRATES: Tell me, then: is the universal fire nourished
* and generated and ruled by the fire in us? Or is the opposite
the case, that the fire in me and in you — in all creatures, in
fact — owes all this to that other fire?

PROTARCHUS: Your question doesn't even deserve an
answer.

d SOCRATES: Right. In fact I imagine you'll say that the
same goes for the earth down here in creatures and the earth in
the universe, and will make the same sort of reply for all the
other components I asked about a short while ago, won't you?

PROTARCHUS: Any other sort of reply would be a sure
sign of insanity, don't you think?

SOCRATES: Nine times out of ten, yes. Now, please pay
attention to the next step. When we were considering the
synthesis of all the components we've just mentioned, we used
the term 'body', didn't we?

PROTARCHUS: Of course.

e SOCRATES: So make the same move in the case of what we
call the universe. I mean, it too should be a body, I suppose, in
the same way, since it consists of the same components.

PROTARCHUS: You're quite right.

SOCRATES: So are our bodies entirely dependent on the
universal body for their nourishment and all the properties we
mentioned just now, or is it the other way round?

PROTARCHUS: That's another pointless question, Socrates.

30*a* SOCRATES: Well then, do you think there's any point to
this one?

PROTARCHUS: Which one?

SOCRATES: Are we to say that our bodies are endowed
with souls?

PROTARCHUS: Obviously.

SOCRATES: Where did they get them from, my dear
Protarchus, unless the universal body has a soul? You see, the
universal body has the same features as ours, except that in its
case those features are even more beautiful in every respect.

PROTARCHUS: Obviously they got them from nowhere else, Socrates.

SOCRATES: Right: for there are present in *everything* those four familiar things – limit, indeterminacy, that which is integrated, and the fourth class, the class of causation; and in *our* *b* case the class of causation engenders soul,[1] instils exercise and treatment for physical ailments, devises remedies suitable for each situation and, in short, gains the title of complete and perfect wisdom as a healer; and there are present in the universe as a whole the *same* physical components, in large amounts and in beautiful and pure form besides. Given all this, you are right, because we are not of course entertaining the idea that the cause has failed to ensure that these physical components are in the finest and most admirable condition possible.

PROTARCHUS: Quite. It would be utterly illogical to *c* think such a thing.

SOCRATES: So if that won't do, we'll be nearer the mark if we stand by our argument and say what we've often said: that there is considerable indeterminacy in the universe, and sufficient limit, and over them an excellent cause which regulates and coordinates the years and seasons and months, and which has every right to be called wisdom and intellect.[2]

---

1. It is important to realize that when the class of causation is said to 'engender' soul, this means that soul (or, strictly, the wisdom and intellect of the soul) is itself a cause, just as the plurality of types that the class of indeterminacy 'engendered' at 26c are each a type of indeterminate. What a class as a whole 'engenders' is itself a member of that class. Without this the argument would be incoherent, as the conclusion that Plato wants, that intellect is itself a cause, would not follow if intellect was not said *here* to be a member of that class.

2. In short, this somewhat loose argument is this: if our body, which is inferior, is looked after by a cause, then how much more must the universal body be looked after by one. This is done by the regularity of the seasons, etc., which, as in fact we could have inferred from 26a–b and 27a–b, must be the action of a cause. Regularity implies intellect at work; therefore intellect causes the universal body's health just as it causes the health of man's body; therefore the universe has a soul. See also *Timaeus* 31b–37c on the body and soul of the universe and on the 'health' of the universal body.

PROTARCHUS: Yes, every right.

SOCRATES: But wisdom and intellect can never occur without soul.

PROTARCHUS: No.

d   SOCRATES: Therefore you will attribute to Zeus[1] a kingly soul and a kingly intellect, because of his function as cause; and to the other deities other fine qualities, suitable for each one's preferred title[2].

PROTARCHUS: Quite so.

SOCRATES: Now, I don't want you thinking that this argument is at all irrelevant, Protarchus; on the contrary, in the first place it supports the men of old who declared that intellect rules the universe.

PROTARCHUS: Yes, it does.

SOCRATES: And it has also answered my question: intel-
*e** lect belongs to the class we said is the cause of anything. And this was one of our four. So here at last is our answer, as I imagine you can now see.

PROTARCHUS: I hadn't appreciated before that you had arrived at the answer, but I can see quite well enough that you have.

SOCRATES: Well, Protarchus, it's sometimes a pleasant change from donnishness not to argue too seriously.[3]

PROTARCHUS: You're right.

31*a* * SOCRATES: I presume, my friend, that the discussion has made more or less reasonably clear to us to which class intellect belongs, and what its particular function is.

PROTARCHUS: Yes, it has.

SOCRATES: And the class to which pleasure belongs became equally clear some time ago.

PROTARCHUS: Indeed it did.

---

1. As ruler of the universe.

2. See p. 53 n.2.

3. Plato admits that he has hardly provided a step-by-step syllogistic argument. As the paraphrase of the argument on p. 83 shows, it is more a profession of faith than a logical argument.

SOCRATES: Let's bear in mind, then, the following facts about them both: intellect was found to be of the same family as the cause, and may be said to belong to that class; but pleasure was found to be indeterminate in itself, and to belong to the class in which, by itself, there is not and never will be any definite beginning, middle or end.

PROTARCHUS: How could we forget it? *b*

SOCRATES: The next step is for us to see where, and under what circumstances, each of them arises when it does. First consider pleasure. Just as we took it first to find out to which class it belongs, so we will also take it first now. We'll never be able to examine pleasure adequately, however, without also considering pain.

PROTARCHUS: Well, if that's the way to proceed, let's do so.

SOCRATES: I wonder if you share my view about their origin?

PROTARCHUS: What is it? *c*

SOCRATES: It seems to me that both pain and pleasure, in the natural course of events, arise in the integrated class.[1]

PROTARCHUS: Please could you remind us, Socrates, which of the previously mentioned classes you mean by the integrated one.

SOCRATES: Really, Protarchus! I'll do so to the best of my ability.

PROTARCHUS: Thanks.

SOCRATES: We must understand the integrated class to be the third of the four we discussed.

PROTARCHUS: The one you discussed after indeterminacy and limit, in which you placed health and, I think, harmony too?

SOCRATES: Exactly. But now pay the closest attention. *d*
PROTARCHUS: Go on.

SOCRATES: My position is that *this* is what happens to

1. This does not contradict the statement that pleasure and pain belong to the indeterminate class: the mixed class is the place of their *origin*.

85

creatures when our physical harmony is being dissolved: at the precise moment of the dissolution of the natural state there occurs the onset of pain.

PROTARCHUS: That's very plausible.

SOCRATES: But when harmony is being restored, and the natural state of harmony is approached, then pleasure arises.[1] This will do, if we have to make as brief a summary as possible about such important issues.

e PROTARCHUS: I think you're right, Socrates, so let's keep to the same formulation, but let's try to make it even clearer.

SOCRATES: In that case, it is easiest to understand things which are conspicuous by being everyday occurrences, isn't it?

PROTARCHUS: What sort of things?

SOCRATES: Hunger, surely, is dissolution and pain?

PROTARCHUS: Yes.

SOCRATES: But eating, the recurrence of replenishment, is pleasure?

PROTARCHUS: Yes.

SOCRATES: Again, thirst is disruption and pain, but when
32*a* liquid replenishes what was formerly parched, that is pleasure. And again, the unnatural disintegration or dissolution which constitutes the experience of stifling heat, is pain; but the contrary restoration and cooling which is congruent with the natural state, is pleasure.

PROTARCHUS: Quite so.

SOCRATES: And the unnatural coagulation of a creature's liquid by freezing, is pain; but when the liquids approach normality again by dispersing, this process is congruent with the natural state, and is pleasure. In short, see if you find the following statement fair: when a living organism – which, as I
b * said before,[2] is a natural product of indeterminacy and limit – when this is disrupted, the disruption is pain; but on the other

---

1. In a natural, equilibriated condition the soul (all sensations are psychic; see 33d) is not experiencing any pleasure or pain (see 32d–33c). 'Pleasure' is a desirable sensation because it is a motion *towards* natural harmony.

2. 30a–c: the word translated 'living' is literally 'ensouled' (*empsuchon*).

hand the reverse process towards the essential nature of such organisms is in all cases pleasure.[1]

PROTARCHUS: Granted: I think that gives the general idea, at least.

SOCRATES: Well then, may we say that one sort of pain and pleasure consists of this pair of experiences?[2]

PROTARCHUS: We may.

SOCRATES: Well, consider what happens in the soul when it anticipates these experiences by itself: the part of the soul *c* which anticipates future pleasures is pleased and confident; but the part which looks to future pains is fearful and distressed.

PROTARCHUS: Quite; so this is another kind of pleasure and pain, the kind which occurs in the soul by itself, without the body, through anticipation.

SOCRATES: Precisely. Now, as I see it, I think we'll be able to use these experiences, when both of them are apparently pure,[3] that is, not a mixture of pleasure and pain, to get clear on whether *every* pleasure is to be welcomed or whether *d* this accolade is to be granted to another of the groups we've mentioned, while pleasure and pain – like heat and cold and so on – are only *sometimes* to be welcomed, on the grounds that they are not good, but that sometimes circumstances are such that some of them assume the character of goods.[4]

PROTARCHUS: You're absolutely right: this is the way to resolve the problems of the present inquiry.

---

1. See also *Timaeus* 64a–65a.

2. That sort of pleasure and pain which may be called 'physical'. He does not mean to imply that other kinds of pleasure and pain will not be seen on the model of depletion and replenishment.

3. That is, physical and psychic pleasures: cf. 51b ff. (Pure pains are not discussed.) The qualification 'apparently' is inserted by Plato because it turns out that even pure pleasures involve preceding pain, though this pain is imperceptible.

4. This long-winded sentence summarizes the rest of the dialogue. It will turn out that the group consisting of Socrates' candidates is to be 'welcomed' *in toto* (62a–d), but that most pleasures are 'impure' and therefore to be denied access to the good life (63d–e).

SOCRATES: Here's the first point for us to consider, then:
e if what we said is true – that pain is the disruption of an organism and pleasure its restoration – then what about an organism which is neither being disrupted nor restored? Let's consider the condition of any creature in such circumstances. Concentrate, and tell me: isn't it absolutely inevitable that every creature, on such occasions, is neither in any pain, nor is he feeling the slightest trace of pleasure?

PROTARCHUS: Yes, inevitably.

SOCRATES: So isn't this a third state, distinct from both
33*a* pleasure and pain?

PROTARCHUS: Of course.

SOCRATES: Be sure to bear it in mind, then: a great deal depends on whether or not we do so, where the assessment of pleasure is concerned. But if you have no objection, let's investigate this state a little.

PROTARCHUS: To what effect?

* SOCRATES: You realize that were one to choose the rational life, there's nothing to prevent his living like that.

PROTARCHUS: You mean living his life free from pleasure
b and pain?

SOCRATES: Yes. When we were comparing the forms of life we said, I seem to remember, that whoever chose the life of intellect and reason should have not the slightest trace of enjoyment.[1]

PROTARCHUS: Yes, that was stressed.

SOCRATES: So that's how it would be for him; and probably nobody would be surprised to find that it is the most divine of all the forms of life.

PROTARCHUS: It *is* unlikely that the gods feel pleasure or the opposite.

SOCRATES: Highly unlikely; at any rate, both are unseem-

1. See 21d–e. This reference does not mean that such a life *is* after all humanly possible; the point is that the only 'organism' which could choose such a life is a god, because gods are the only beings which are 'neither being disrupted nor restored'. Nevertheless, the divine life can be held to be ideally desirable, as it is at 55a.

ly for them.[1] We'll go into this again later, however, if it is at all relevant to the discussion,[2] and we'll add it to the credit of *c* intellect as regards the second prize, if we cannot do so as regards the first.

PROTARCHUS: Very well.

SOCRATES: Now, all pleasures of the second kind, which we said belong just to the soul, arise thanks to memory.

PROTARCHUS: How?

SOCRATES: If we are to find a way to explain these matters properly, it looks as though we must first consider the nature of memory, and probably, even before memory, the nature of sensation.

PROTARCHUS: What do you mean? *d*

SOCRATES: Consider this hypothesis about any physical feeling: some are extinguished in the body before they penetrate to the soul, and the soul remains unaffected; but others penetrate both and create a sort of shock, as it were, which is peculiar to each part, and yet common to both.[3]

PROTARCHUS: I accept that hypothesis.

SOCRATES: So how may we express this best? What about if, when the feelings do not penetrate both, we were to say that the soul is oblivious; and when they do, that it is not oblivious.

PROTARCHUS: Yes, that'll do. *e*

SOCRATES: Now, you mustn't suppose that when I use the word 'oblivion' I mean the phenomenon of forgetfulness.

---

1. Aristotle, on the other hand, says that god feels 'one simple pleasure for ever' (*Nicomachean Ethics* 1154b 25).

2. As presumably it is not, since the topic is not raised again.

3. Peculiar to each because physical shock must differ from psychic shock as the body differs from the soul; but common to both because it is the same shock from the same source. See also *Timaeus* 64a–c for a physiological explanation of sensation. Plato assumes the usual Greek philosophical notion of the soul in which, apart from containing the faculties of emotion, thought, memory, etc. (and apart from being the immortal part of man), it is also that which experiences sensation. Strictly speaking, the body is merely an inert lump of matter.

Forgetfulness is loss of memory, but in the situation now under consideration there has as yet been no memory: it's absurd to talk of loss of something which does not exist or has not yet occurred. Don't you agree?

PROTARCHUS: Naturally.

SOCRATES: So just make a change in the terminology.

PROTARCHUS: What?

SOCRATES: At present you are saying that the soul is oblivious when it is unaffected by physical shocks; but instead of 34a 'oblivion', use the term 'insensibility'.

PROTARCHUS: I see.

SOCRATES: When the soul and the body together share a single experience, however, and are moved together, if you call *this* movement 'sensation', you'll be on safe ground.

PROTARCHUS: That's perfectly true.

SOCRATES: Do we now understand what we mean by 'sensation'?

PROTARCHUS: Of course.

SOCRATES: And it would be right – at least I think it would – to say that memory is 'preservation of sensation'.

b PROTARCHUS: Yes, you'd be right.

SOCRATES: Isn't recollection different from memory?

PROTARCHUS: Presumably.

SOCRATES: And isn't the difference this?

PROTARCHUS: What?

SOCRATES: Don't we call recollection what the soul does internally, without the body, when it resuscitates, as thoroughly as possible, the experiences it once shared with the body?

PROTARCHUS: Yes.

SOCRATES: Moreover, suppose the soul has lost the memory of a sensation or of a piece of information but later recovers c* it again internally: that counts as recollection too, of memories, doesn't it?[1]

PROTARCHUS: Right.

. 1. If this is supposed to pinpoint the difference between recollection and memory by stating that memory can be the *object* of recollection, then Plato has made a rather elementary mistake here. He has set out to distinguish recol-

SOCRATES: Now, there's a purpose behind all this discussion.

PROTARCHUS: What?

SOCRATES: To gain the best and clearest possible view of pleasure in the soul – the soul without the body; and to do the same for desire. Desire too is likely to be clarified by these points.

PROTARCHUS: So now let's get on with this next subject, Socrates.

SOCRATES: If our discussion of the origin and character of pleasure is to be complete it must, it seems, include the examination of many things; and now, as a further preliminary, *d* it looks as though we have to understand the nature and basis of desire.

PROTARCHUS: Let's examine it, then. We have nothing to lose.

SOCRATES: Oh, yes, we have, Protarchus. If we achieve our goal, we'll lose our ignorance of the subject!

PROTARCHUS: *Touché*! But let's try to keep things moving.

SOCRATES: Well, weren't we saying just now that hunger, thirst and so on and so forth are desires?[1] *e*

PROTARCHUS: Certainly.

SOCRATES: So what is the feature common to these states, so very different as they are, by virtue of which we called them all by a single name?

PROTARCHUS: Heavens, Socrates! That's a difficult one. But we must reply all the same.

SOCRATES: So let's resume exactly where we left off.

---

lection from the faculty of memory, but he confuses the faculty of memory ('he has a good memory') with memory in the sense of the thing remembered ('he had a vivid memory of the event'). The latter can be lost but not the former. What Plato wants to say is, for instance, that memory is the faculty, recollection the use of the faculty; and it is probably a better interpretation of the passage to suppose that he means this to be clear enough from what is said about the faculty of memory in 34a and recollection in 34b–c.

1. 31e–32b, but he didn't call them desires at the time.

PROTARCHUS: Where was that?

SOCRATES: We use, when appropriate, the expression 'he is thirsty', don't we?

PROTARCHUS: Of course.

SOCRATES: Which is to say, 'he has a lack'?

PROTARCHUS: Naturally.

SOCRATES: Well, is thirst desire?

PROTARCHUS: Yes, for drink.

35a SOCRATES: For drink, or for replenishment by drink?

PROTARCHUS: For replenishment, I think.

SOCRATES: It seems, then, that if anyone has a lack, he desires the opposite to his present state: I mean, whoever has a lack craves replenishment.

PROTARCHUS: Yes, that's very clear.

SOCRATES: Fine. But what about someone who has a lack for the first time? Is there any way in which he can comprehend replenishment, by sensation or by memory? Can he comprehend what he is not experiencing at the time and has never experienced in the past?

PROTARCHUS: Of course not.[1]

b SOCRATES: But *desire* does have an object, as we said.

PROTARCHUS: Of course.

SOCRATES: The object is not the present experience of thirst: thirst is a lack, and the thirsty man desires replenishment.

PROTARCHUS: Yes.

SOCRATES: So some part of the thirsty man can somehow comprehend replenishment.

PROTARCHUS: Necessarily.

SOCRATES: It cannot be his body, given that it is experiencing the lack.

1. Plato is trying to locate the difference he sees between lack and desire; a new-born baby, for instance, can feel a lack, but cannot be said to desire, since desiring implies an object, and the object is established by memory of what the remedy is for that particular lack. But the baby, while it feels the pain of the lack, cannot yet have knowledge of what will remedy it.

PROTARCHUS: Quite.

SOCRATES: That only leaves his soul; and what else could it use to comprehend replenishment but memory? c

PROTARCHUS: Nothing else, I suppose.

SOCRATES: Are we, then, in a position to see what this argument entails?

PROTARCHUS: What's that?

SOCRATES: The denial that desire is physical.

PROTARCHUS: Why?

SOCRATES: Because it shows that every living creature always strives for the opposite to his present state.

PROTARCHUS: Certainly.

SOCRATES: The tendency towards the opposite to the present state demonstrates, I think, that there is memory of the various opposites to the various current states.

PROTARCHUS: Yes, it does.

SOCRATES: Therefore, by showing that it is memory that d provides the impulse towards the objects of desire, the argument is declaring that all drive, desire and authority, in every living creature, belong to the soul.

PROTARCHUS: Absolutely right.

SOCRATES: Therefore the argument proves that the human body plays no part in thirst, hunger and so on.[1]

PROTARCHUS: True indeed.

SOCRATES: Moreover, there's another point these same considerations bring to our attention: the argument seems to me to adumbrate a certain way of life spent in these states.

PROTARCHUS: In what states? What sort of life are you e talking about?

SOCRATES: A life spent in replenishment and lack and, generally, in everything which contributes to the preservation and destruction of creatures; a life spent in passing from one state to the other, from pain, say, to subsequent pleasure.

PROTARCHUS: Quite.

---

1. Here we have to understand thirst and hunger to stand not just for the lack, but for the total experience, including desire, etc.

SOCRATES: But what about when one is in between these states?

PROTARCHUS: What do you mean, 'in between'?

SOCRATES: When the feeling is one of pain, but there is memory of the pleasure whose occurrence would put an end to the pain, but the replenishment itself has not yet taken place. What is happening then? Are we to say that he is in between 36a the states or not?

PROTARCHUS: We have to.

SOCRATES: We can't really say *tout court* that he's either in a painful or a pleasant condition, can we?

PROTARCHUS: Heavens, no! On the contrary, his condition is one of double pain: not only is there the physical feeling, but also there's unsatisfied expectation in his soul.

SOCRATES: What do you mean, Protarchus? Double pain? Aren't there times when, though experiencing a lack, we have distinct hope of replenishment, while at other times, on the b contrary, there is no such hope?

PROTARCHUS: Certainly.

SOCRATES: So don't you think that someone who is expecting replenishment feels pleasure thanks to his memory but, since he is also experiencing the lack at the same time, is ∗ simultaneously feeling pain?

PROTARCHUS: Inevitably.

SOCRATES: Therefore at such a time man and all other creatures feel simultaneous pain and pleasure.

PROTARCHUS: I suppose you're right.

SOCRATES: But what about when, while experiencing a lack, he has *no* hope of replenishment coming his way? Isn't it then that his pain would be doubled? Here, as you thought, is c the experience you noticed just recently of nothing but pain.[1]

PROTARCHUS: Very true, Socrates.

1. Protarchus' mistake in 36a was not in thinking that physical pain plus unsatisfied expectation is double pain, but in locating truly unsatisfied expectation in the experience Socrates was talking about.

SOCRATES: Now, there's a use to which we can put our examination of these experiences.

PROTARCHUS: What?

SOCRATES: Shall we say that these pains and pleasures are true or false? Or that some are true, some not?[1]

PROTARCHUS: But Socrates, how can pleasures or pains be false?

SOCRATES: But Protarchus, how can fears be true or false, or expectations, or beliefs?

PROTARCHUS: I would agree, of course, that beliefs can be, but not the rest.   *d*

SOCRATES: Why? Oh, but the chances are that we're embarking on quite a lengthy argument.

PROTARCHUS: True.

SOCRATES: Like father, like son.[2] But we must see whether the issue is relevant to matters we have already discussed.[3]

PROTARCHUS: I suppose so.

SOCRATES: Our rule, then, is to welcome length except when it would serve no purpose.

PROTARCHUS: Right.

SOCRATES: Now, there are no questions I find so per-   *e* petually puzzling as the ones we've just asked. So tell me what *you* think. Aren't some pleasures false, while others are true?

PROTARCHUS: How could they be?

SOCRATES: So your claim is that no one ever – even if he's

---

1. *Republic* 580–587b is worth comparing with the discussion of false pleasures in the *Philebus*.

2. Protarchus' father was called Callias (19b). But since we do not know if he is to be identified with any of the Calliases we know of, it is difficult to make sense of this remark. Possibly, on the other hand, Socrates is referring to Philebus as Protarchus' figurative father, in the sense that Protarchus has inherited his thesis (11a). If that is so, then Socrates might be saying that Protarchus, like Philebus, is showing a tendency to try and avoid a long argument.

3. Especially the question of the value of pleasure.

asleep, or even if he's awake but insane or delirious – thinks he is pleased, but really isn't at all, or alternatively thinks he is in pain, but really is not.

PROTARCHUS: That, Socrates, is precisely the assumption we're *all* making.[1]

SOCRATES: But is it right? Shouldn't we consider whether or not it is?

PROTARCHUS: I think we should.

37a SOCRATES: So let's make what we just said about pleasure and belief even clearer: there is such a thing as belief, isn't there?

PROTARCHUS: Yes.

SOCRATES: And as pleasure?

PROTARCHUS: Yes.

SOCRATES: Moreover, belief has an object, doesn't it?

PROTARCHUS: Of course.

SOCRATES: As does pleasure too?

PROTARCHUS: Certainly.

SOCRATES: So whoever has a belief, whether or not it is correct, never fails to have a genuine belief.

b PROTARCHUS: How could he?

SOCRATES: And whoever feels pleasure, whether or not it is correct, clearly never fails to have a genuine pleasure.

PROTARCHUS: Yes, that's so too.

SOCRATES: In other words, what we have to consider is how belief tends to be false as well as true, but pleasure only true, while both equally have the property of being genuine cases of believing and being pleased.

PROTARCHUS: Yes, that's what we have to consider.

SOCRATES: Is this what you mean we should consider – that in the case of belief, falsity and truth are attributable to it,
c with the result that it isn't just belief that occurs, but belief with one quality or the other?

1. Protarchus enlists the support of the other people present at the discussion. But it was never Plato's belief that the majority opinion was necessarily right.

PROTARCHUS: Yes.

SOCRATES: We must also agree on whether, while some things are qualifiable, pleasure and pain are just what they are, with no qualities.

PROTARCHUS: Obviously.

SOCRATES: Well, at any rate, it's not difficult to see that they *are* also qualifiable: we said some time ago that both of them, both pleasures and pains, become great and small, even extremely so. [1]

PROTARCHUS: Absolutely.   d

SOCRATES: If they gain the quality of worthlessness, Protarchus, won't we say that the result is a worthless belief, or a worthless pleasure?

PROTARCHUS: Of course, Socrates.

SOCRATES: And what if they gain the quality of accuracy or the opposite? Take accuracy: won't we talk of accurate belief, and likewise for pleasure?

PROTARCHUS: Necessarily.

SOCRATES: And if a mistake is made about the object of   e
belief, shouldn't we agree that the belief which makes the mistake is not accurate, and does not judge correctly?

PROTARCHUS: Of course.

SOCRATES: And if we also find a pain or a pleasure being mistaken in its object, will we call it correct or worthwhile or assign it *any* term of approval?

PROTARCHUS: No, we couldn't, if pleasure *is* capable of such mistakes.

SOCRATES: Now, pleasure often seems to accompany false belief rather than true belief.

PROTARCHUS: Of course. And in such a situation it is the belief that we call false, Socrates, not the pleasure; no one 38a
would ever say that the pleasure itself was false.

SOCRATES: How keenly you're defending the cause of pleasure now, Protarchus!

---

1. See 27e–28a.

PROTARCHUS: Not really. I'm just repeating what I've heard.

SOCRATES: Given that we all get pleasure not only when we have correct belief and knowledge, but often when we are deceived and ignorant, is there no difference at all between the two cases?

b   PROTARCHUS: Yes, there's probably quite a bit of difference.

SOCRATES: So let's go on to consider the difference between them.

PROTARCHUS: We are in your hands.

SOCRATES: Well, this is the direction I shall take us in.

PROTARCHUS: What?

SOCRATES: Aren't we affirming that both false and true belief exist?

PROTARCHUS: We are.

SOCRATES: And, as we were saying just now, pleasure and pain often accompany them – true and false belief, I mean.

PROTARCHUS: Certainly.

SOCRATES: Whenever belief and the attempt to form a definite opinion occur, don't they arise out of memory and perception?[1]

c   PROTARCHUS: Indeed they do.

SOCRATES: In other words, don't we think that what necessarily happens is this?

PROTARCHUS: What?

SOCRATES: Imagine someone who is far away from the things he is looking at and so isn't seeing them very well. Wouldn't you say that, in general, he's bound to want to make up his mind about what it is he's seeing?

PROTARCHUS: I would.

SOCRATES: Next, then, mightn't he ask himself the following question?

PROTARCHUS: What?

---

1. The same word (*aisthēsis*) has now to be translated 'perception' that was earlier translated 'sensation'. For Plato, perception is just a special form of sensation.

SOCRATES: 'I can see something standing by the rock under the tree – but what on earth is it?' Don't you think *d* that this might pass through his mind as he looks down on this kind of scene?

PROTARCHUS: Of course.

SOCRATES: And mightn't our subject next reply to himself – and let's suppose he gets it right – 'it's a man'?

PROTARCHUS: He might indeed.

SOCRATES: On the other hand, if he was mistaken, he might perhaps say that what he is seeing is a shepherds' statue.

PROTARCHUS: Quite.

SOCRATES: One possibility is that he could have a companion, to whom he might say the same things he previously said to himself, but now put into audible speech. If that happens, then what we were previously calling belief has become a statement, hasn't it?[1]

PROTARCHUS: Of course.

SOCRATES: Alternatively, if these thoughts occur when there's nobody with him, he might go around for quite a long time without externalizing them.

PROTARCHUS: Quite.

SOCRATES: Well then, I wonder if you see it as I do?

PROTARCHUS: How?

SOCRATES: I think that on such occasions the soul resembles a book.

PROTARCHUS: How?

SOCRATES: When memory coincides with perception, it *39a* and other faculties relevant to these experiences seem to me to write words, as it were, in the soul.[2] When this

1. See also *Theaetetus* 189e–190a and *Sophist* 263e–264a for belief as internal speech.

2. 'Writing words in the soul' is identifying an object as, say, a scarecrow. Memory is relevant as the object could not be so identified unless it, or something similar, had been perceived in the past, and remembered. The part of the 'other faculties' is less clear; perhaps they are, e.g., common sense, which confirms that it is likely to be a statue in such a rural setting: the Greeks commonly erected various religious objects in the countryside.

* experience[1] writes the truth, it gives rise to true belief and our internal statements are true; but when this secretary of ours records what is false, the resulting statements are the opposite of true.

PROTARCHUS: Yes, I do agree with you. I accept this
b account.

SOCRATES: You have yet to accept the presence of another member of the soul's work-force on these occasions.

PROTARCHUS: Who?

SOCRATES: An artist, who turns the secretary's words into images in the soul.

PROTARCHUS: What do you mean? What are we to say this one does, and at what stage of the process?

SOCRATES: When the contact between the relevant beliefs and statements, and the sight or whichever form of perception it was, is broken, then, in a way, internal images
c are formed of the things which were believed and stated. Isn't that what happens?

PROTARCHUS: Certainly.

SOCRATES: So aren't the images of true beliefs and statements true, but of false, false.

PROTARCHUS: Absolutely.

SOCRATES: If we've been right so far, then there's an additional point to consider.

PROTARCHUS: What?

SOCRATES: Whether this experience is restricted to the present and the past but is not concerned with the future.

PROTARCHUS: It must apply equally to all times.

d SOCRATES: In fact didn't we say earlier[2] that the pleasures and pains of the soul by itself might occur before the pleasures and pains of the body? Doesn't it then follow that where the future is concerned we can feel pleasure or pain before the event?

PROTARCHUS: Perfectly true.

SOCRATES: So what about the internal writings and pic-

1. The conglomerate of memory, perception, etc.
2. 32b–c, 36b.

tures which we recently postulated? Are they only concerned with the past and the present, not with the future? *e*

PROTARCHUS: They are very much concerned with the future.

SOCRATES: Why do you say 'very much'? Is it because in this case they are all *hopes* for the future and, after all, we spend our whole lives as full of hope as can be?

PROTARCHUS: That's precisely it.

SOCRATES: Well, we've got so far, but answer me this too.

PROTARCHUS: What?

SOCRATES: Isn't a man who is just, devout and good in all respects, favoured by the gods?[1]

PROTARCHUS: Naturally.

SOCRATES: But the opposite is true for a man who is unjust and utterly evil? 40*a*

PROTARCHUS: Of course.

SOCRATES: As we were just saying, however, it's a fact that *every* man is full of all sorts of hopes, isn't it?

PROTARCHUS: Of course.

SOCRATES: And there are statements in *each* of us, which we are calling hopes?

PROTARCHUS: Yes.

SOCRATES: In particular, there are the pictured images: often someone sees himself getting an incredible amount of money, and he sees the pleasures to be gained from it; he sees himself in the picture too, enjoying himself immensely.[2]

1. The moralistic tone of this and the following lines is striking. Plato could have made his point equally well by saying merely that anticipated pleasures sometimes come to pass, sometimes not – i.e. without mentioning good and bad men. Perhaps his purpose is to counter the common mood of Greek pessimism, in which unjust men often prosper, with a more optimistic viewpoint and one which sees the gods as more moral.

2. I take it that these are the hopes of a bad man. The good man, being more restrained (45d–e) will make more modest demands on the gods' good will, and will *therefore* have true hopes. Thus Plato implicitly avoids a danger in his moralizing: at first sight it looks as though we could recognize a 'good' man by whether his hopes, however sadistic or whatever, were fulfilled. But in fact the good man will not have any such hopes.

b PROTARCHUS: Of course.

SOCRATES: We have a choice, then: either we are to affirm that, because they are favoured by the gods, good men invariably get statements and pictures which are true, and that bad men invariably get the opposite, or we are to deny it.[1] Which do you think we should do?

PROTARCHUS: I think we should confidently affirm it.

SOCRATES: Therefore, though bad men too get just as many pictured pleasures, these pleasures are, it seems, false.[2]

PROTARCHUS: Of course.

c SOCRATES: So most of the pleasures worthless men feel are false; those of good men, true.

PROTARCHUS: It's impossible to disagree with you.

SOCRATES: So this argument shows that there *are* pleasures in men's souls which are false, but they are rather ridiculous copies of true pleasures. And the same goes for pains.

PROTARCHUS: Yes, there are.

SOCRATES: Well, we found that anyone who ever believes anything at all does genuinely have a belief, but that nevertheless the object of the belief might not be the case now, might never have been, and might even not be in the future.

PROTARCHUS: Certainly.

d SOCRATES: And we found, I think, that these were the circumstances which, when they occur, cause belief to be false and make one believe falsely, didn't we?

PROTARCHUS: Yes.

SOCRATES: What about pains and pleasures, then? In the same circumstances, shouldn't we attribute a corresponding condition to them?

1. Unlike Aristotle (*De Interpretatione* 9), Plato sees no difficulty in calling a *present* statement true or false whether in the *future* the event occurs or not.

2. Plato needs another premiss here before he can draw the conclusion of the next sentence. He has argued that the pleasures *in* the picture are false, but this is non-controversial, since they are part of the belief which is agreed to be false. Since he has undertaken to show that an actual experience of pleasure can be false, he needs in addition, e.g.: 'And the pleasures in the picture provoke currently experienced pleasures' (cf. 39d).

PROTARCHUS: Why?

SOCRATES: Because we found that anyone who is ever pleased at all – even if quite groundlessly – is genuinely feeling pleasure, but that the object of his pleasure might not be the case now, occasionally might never have been, and often, perhaps most often, might never take place in the future.

PROTARCHUS: Once again, Socrates, it's impossible to *e* deny that this is so.

SOCRATES: What about fear, anger and so on? Won't the same argument be valid for them too, that they are all sometimes false?

PROTARCHUS: Certainly.

SOCRATES: Now, would we call beliefs worthless and useless except when they are false?   *

PROTARCHUS: No.

SOCRATES: Nor, in my opinion, would we find that pleasures are worthless unless they are false.

PROTARCHUS: No, you've got it quite the wrong way 41*a* round, Socrates: I don't think pains and pleasures can be taken to be particularly worthless thanks to falsity, not unless they meet with a great deal of worthlessness from elsewhere as well.

SOCRATES: Well, let's postpone the discussion of worthless pleasures which stem from worthlessness until it seems appropriate.[1] But, to return to false pleasures, there's another way in which we all too often experience them: we ought to discuss this, since it will presumably support our verdicts.[2] *b*

PROTARCHUS: Of course it will, if there *are* any other false pleasures.

---

1. 45a–e is the closest he comes to an explicit discussion of worthlessness in pleasure: there certain mixed pleasures are associated with a worthless physical or mental condition. But, implicitly, the whole idea of pleasure being mixed with pain provides the sort of grounds on which Protarchus, as a hedonist, could agree that pleasures are worthless: a hedonist cannot see pain in any other way.

2. An acknowledgement that the describing of certain pleasures as false is being taken to be relevant to the verdicts about pleasure and reason and their relative priority.

SOCRATES: There are indeed, Protarchus, or at least I think there are. But we can't leave this opinion of mine untested, I trust, until the matter's settled.

PROTARCHUS: Right.

SOCRATES: So let's take up our positions for this next round in the argument.

PROTARCHUS: Yes, let's go.

SOCRATES: Well, it's worth remembering what we said a

c little earlier: that what are known as desires are such that when they occur, what the body feels is distinct and separate from what the soul feels.

PROTARCHUS: We remember: that's what we said.

SOCRATES: Didn't we find, in fact, that the soul desires states opposite to the current physical ones, and feels pleasure or pain according to how the body is affected?

PROTARCHUS: Yes, that's what we found.

SOCRATES: So work out what's happening in this situation.

PROTARCHUS: No, you tell me, please.

d SOCRATES: Well, what happens when this is the case, is that pain and pleasure overlap and, opposite though they are, are perceived simultaneously, side by side, as I explained recently.[1]

PROTARCHUS: Yes, that seems right.

SOCRATES: Now, another proposition we agreed on before is relevant here, isn't it?

PROTARCHUS: Which one?

SOCRATES: That both pleasure and pain admit 'more and less', that is, that they are among the indeterminates.

PROTARCHUS: That was the proposition; what of it?

SOCRATES: What means is there, then, of making a correct assessment of them?

e PROTARCHUS: What do you mean? What assessment?

SOCRATES: I mean if in a situation such as we are describing we want to assess them in the sense of discerning the

1. 36b.

relative size, degree or intensity of the pain compared with the pleasure, or pain with pain, or pleasure with pleasure, as the case may be.

PROTARCHUS: Yes, that's true. That's an assessment we want to make.

SOCRATES: Well now, in the case of sight, if the size of anything is inspected from too far away or too close, the truth is obscured and the consequent belief is false: doesn't the same thing therefore happen in the case of pleasures and pains? 42*a*

PROTARCHUS: Yes, far more than with sight, Socrates.

SOCRATES: So this has turned out to be the opposite to the case we were looking at a little while ago.

PROTARCHUS: What do you mean?

SOCRATES: Previously the beliefs simultaneously infected the pains or pleasures with their own condition of truth or falsity.

PROTARCHUS: Perfectly true. *b*

SOCRATES: But in the present case the pains and pleasures are being inspected, as they alternate and are compared with one another, from too far away or too close, as the case may be. Consequently, the pleasures, when compared with the pains, are assessed as too great and intense; and *vice versa* for the pains, through being compared with pleasures.[1]

---

1. The sort of situation Plato has in mind is this: the immediate pleasure of having an extra pint of beer will result in pain the next morning. But tomorrow morning seems a long way off, and so the pain seems small compared with the immediate pleasure, which in turn seems large *qua* immediate. Here the pain is being viewed 'from too far away' and the pleasure 'from too close'. The opposite case, which is not adumbrated in this paragraph but in the context as a whole, would be, say, the pain of giving up smoking compared with the pleasure of being healthy (and wealthy!): the pleasure seems a long way off and inconsiderable compared with the withdrawal symptoms currently being experienced. This interpretation preserves both the similarity of the passage to *Protagoras* 356a–e and the analogy with sight mentioned in 41e–42a: anything viewed from afar seems small, from too close, large. This sort of false pleasure is the opposite of the previous sort of false pleasure (42a) in that now, instead of belief affecting pleasure, the proximity or distance of the pleasure is affecting one's judgement about its size.

PROTARCHUS: Yes, that must inevitably be the result of this process.

SOCRATES: So each gives the impression of being greater or less than it actually is. If you isolate this unreal impression, you will see that it is mistaken, and you will never dare
c to call correct and true whatever amount of pleasure or pain is involved in this impression.

PROTARCHUS: No, indeed.

SOCRATES: Now, we have found that living beings experience pleasures and pains which seem, and indeed are, false. Next we will see if in our inquiry we come across pleasures and pains whose falsity is even greater.

PROTARCHUS: What do you mean? Which pleasures and pains do you have in mind?

SOCRATES: We've often said, as you know, that when the natural state of any creature is being disrupted by aggregation or disintegration, replenishment or lack, in short
d by any development or decline, the result is pain, discomfort, distress and their cognates.[1]

PROTARCHUS: Yes, we've often said so.

SOCRATES: When the natural state is being restored, however, we satisfied ourselves that this restoration is pleasure.

PROTARCHUS: Right.

SOCRATES: What about when the body is undergoing none of these processes?

PROTARCHUS: But Socrates, can that *ever* be the case?

e SOCRATES: An irrelevant question, Protarchus.

PROTARCHUS: Why?

SOCRATES: Because I can still repeat *my* question.[2]

PROTARCHUS: What question?

---

1. Normally pain is characterized as lack, pleasure as replenishment, as at 31d–32b; but sometimes replenishment will disturb the 'harmony' of the body just as effectively as lack, so it is included here.

2. Socrates takes his question to invite discussion *about* the neutral state, not about whether there is such a state.

SOCRATES: I can still say: 'Just suppose, Protarchus, that this is the case: what conclusion must we draw?'

PROTARCHUS: You mean if the body is not being moved in either direction?

SOCRATES: Precisely.

PROTARCHUS: Well, Socrates, *were* such a situation to occur, obviously there would be no feeling of pleasure or of pain.

SOCRATES: Well said. But I imagine your view is that 43*a* there must always be some process going on in us – indeed, this is the view of the experts: it follows from their assertion that everything is *always* in flux back and forth.[1]

PROTARCHUS: Yes, that's what they say, and their idea seems to deserve serious consideration.

SOCRATES: Of course it does: they're such serious people! Nevertheless, I want to avoid the discussion that's threatening us here; I have an escape-route in mind, so follow me.

PROTARCHUS: I will, if you tell me where.

SOCRATES: First we tell *them* that we accept their theory; but that *still* leaves you with a question to answer: does any *b* living being always perceive everything that happens to it? When some development, or whatever it may be, occurs in us, are we always aware of it, or is just the opposite the case?

PROTARCHUS: Just the opposite, I reckon: we're hardly ever aware of such things.

SOCRATES: So our recent assertion, that changes back and forth produce pleasures and pains, could be improved.

PROTARCHUS: Yes.

SOCRATES: It'll be better and less open to criticism to *c* put it as follows.

1. This is Plato's usual, but partial, interpretation of the Presocratic philosopher Heraclitus and his followers: Heraclitus said (fragment 60): 'The road back and forth is one and the same'; but this was an illustration not just of the flux and mobility of the world, but also of its underlying unity. At *Theaetetus* 152e Plato claims that flux is the view not only of the Heracliteans, but also of a whole host of 'experts'; see also *Sophist* 242d–e, *Cratylus* 440b–d.

PROTARCHUS: How?

SOCRATES: That only *large* changes produce pains and pleasures, but moderate, small ones have no effect on us at all, in either way.

PROTARCHUS: Yes, that's a better formulation than before, Socrates.

SOCRATES: In that case, we can resurrect the life we mentioned just now.[1]

PROTARCHUS: Which one?

SOCRATES: The one we said contains neither pains nor pleasures.

PROTARCHUS: You're absolutely right.

SOCRATES: It follows that we can postulate three modes
d of existence: pleasant, painful and neutral.[2] Do you agree or not?

PROTARCHUS: That's exactly how I would put it: there are three modes of existence.

SOCRATES: So freedom from pain is not the same as pleasure, is it?

PROTARCHUS: Of course not.

SOCRATES: When you hear someone saying that the most pleasant thing of all is to spend one's whole life without pain, what do you suppose he means?[3]

PROTARCHUS: I take him to mean that freedom from pain is pleasant.

e SOCRATES: Now, take any three things, no matter what they are — well, let's use things with rather attractive names: take, for example, gold, silver and some third thing which is neither of these.

PROTARCHUS: All right.

1. He can now maintain both that we are always involved in some process, and that we do not necessarily perceive it.

2. The neutral life is not the same as the divine life of 32d–33c. There it was a matter of a being which was *in fact* not undergoing any processes; here it is a matter merely of not perceiving them, even though they are going on.

3. At *Protagoras* 355a this view is attributed to the majority of mankind.

SOCRATES: Are there any circumstances under which the neutral thing can become either of the others, either gold or silver?

PROTARCHUS: No, there aren't.

SOCRATES: Therefore, strictly, the intermediate life should not be thought or said – whichever is the case – to be pleasant or painful; strictly speaking, that is.

PROTARCHUS: No, it shouldn't.

SOCRATES: Nevertheless, my friend, we do find people 44*a* saying and thinking these things.

PROTARCHUS: Indeed we do.

SOCRATES: Is that because, when they are not feeling pain, they imagine they are actually feeling pleasure?

PROTARCHUS: That's what they say, at any rate.

SOCRATES: Well, if they didn't imagine they were, I don't suppose they'd go on saying it.

PROTARCHUS: I suppose not.

SOCRATES: But their idea about pleasure is false, if freedom from pain is different from pleasure.

PROTARCHUS: We have certainly found them to be different.

SOCRATES: We have a choice, then: are we to stand by our recent assertion that there are three states, or are we to say that there are only two? If only two, we would say that one of them *b* is pain, a bane for man, and the other is relief from pain which is called pleasant because it is good.

PROTARCHUS: I don't see how we can ask ourselves such a thing at this juncture, Socrates.

SOCRATES: That's because you don't see the real enemies Philebus here has, Protarchus.   *

PROTARCHUS: Who do you mean?

SOCRATES: They have the reputation of being pretty shrewd philosophers: they deny that pleasures exist at all!

PROTARCHUS: On what grounds?

SOCRATES: According to them, everything which the *c* Philebuses of this world now call pleasures are cases of release from pain.

PROTARCHUS: Are you suggesting that we believe them, Socrates, or what?

SOCRATES: Not that we believe them, but that we regard them as oracles, as it were,[1] whose insight is not a result of science but of the dourness which is natural to a well-bred character. Their hatred for pleasure is excessive: the fact is, they think, there is nothing wholesome about it at all – it is *d* not actually pleasure that is attractive, but an illusion. So that is how you should regard them, and you should also consider other consequences of their dourness; when you've done that, I'll tell you which pleasures I think are true. Our verdict[2] should be helped by collating what we learn about pleasure from both positions.

PROTARCHUS: Right.

SOCRATES: Let's follow their lead, then, as if they were our allies in a military venture, matching their dourness step for step. I take their meaning to be somewhat as follows. They start with a general question: suppose we wanted to understand the nature of any kind of thing – of hardness, for exam-*e* ple; if we examined the most extreme instances of hardness, would this serve us better than inspection of things low down on the scale of hardness? You've been answering me, Protarchus, so you should answer our dour friends.

PROTARCHUS: Very well. My reply is that we should inspect those with the maximum amount.

SOCRATES: So if we also wanted to understand the nature of pleasure, we should not inspect the slightest pleasures, but *45a* those which are thought to be the very acme of intensity in pleasure.

PROTARCHUS: That is indisputable.

SOCRATES: It's a well-known fact that we find the combination of accessibility and intensity in physical pleasures, don't we?

1. That is, as having insight, but expressing it in an ambiguous or incomplete way.

2. Which of pleasure or reason is superior.

PROTARCHUS: Of course.

SOCRATES: Now, who feels, or rather, comes to feel, pleasure more intensely? Those who are stricken by sickness, or healthy people? Careful now; we might make a mistake if we rush into an answer: I mean, we would probably have replied, *b* 'healthy people'.

PROTARCHUS: Yes, we probably would have.

SOCRATES: But isn't it the case that the greater the preceding desire, the greater the pleasure?

PROTARCHUS: That's true.

SOCRATES: Well, don't those who are gripped by fever and so on suffer more from thirst, cold and all the usual physical complaints? Aren't they more familiar with lack? Don't they get greater pleasures from replenishment? That is undeniably *
true, isn't it?

PROTARCHUS: It certainly seems to be, put that way.

SOCRATES: Would you think we were right, then, if we said that it is to disease, not health, that anyone wishing to see the greatest pleasures must direct his attention? Please don't think that I'm intending to ask you whether seriously ill people feel a greater *number* of pleasures than healthy people; you must realize that I'm looking for *size* of pleasure, and the location of any instance of intensity of degree. This follows from what we said: that we must understand the nature of pleasure and what those who utterly deny its existence take it to be.

PROTARCHUS: Don't worry: I'm just about keeping up *d* with your argument.

SOCRATES: Here's your chance to prove as much, Protarchus, by answering this question: from what you have observed, does an unbalanced or a self-controlled life contain greater pleasures? Think before you answer; I mean greater in intensity and degree, not in number.

PROTARCHUS: I *know* what you mean. I've noticed a great difference between them: self-controlled men, of course, are restrained in whatever they do by their adherence to the proverbial recommendation of 'nothing in excess'.[1] But fools and *e*

1. A saying attributed in various forms to all the seven sages of Greece, and

those who are unbalanced to the point of insanity are pawns of intense pleasure which drives them to scandalous behaviour.

SOCRATES: A good reply. And if this is so, then clearly intensity of both pleasure and pain is to be found not in a good state of body and soul, but in a worthless one.

PROTARCHUS: Quite so.

SOCRATES: The proper course, then, is to examine a selection of such pleasures and pains to see what it is about them that makes them so intense.

46a PROTARCHUS: Yes, we must.

SOCRATES: Consider, then, what it is about the pleasures found in the following ailments.

PROTARCHUS: Which ailments?

SOCRATES: Rather indecent ones, the pleasures which our dour friends, as we called them, utterly detest.

PROTARCHUS: Which pleasures?

SOCRATES: For example relieving pruritus and other such ailments which require no treatment besides rubbing. How in all honesty are we to describe this feeling? Are we to call it
* pleasant or painful, when it is a mixture of both?
* PROTARCHUS: You certainly seem to have chosen an unsavoury example, Socrates.

b SOCRATES: Well, I haven't been trying to gratify Philebus with my argument. No, these and others like them are the pleasures we need to understand, Protarchus, otherwise we won't be able to conclude our present investigation.

PROTARCHUS: So we should continue with others of the same group.

SOCRATES: Do you mean the mixed group?

PROTARCHUS: Yes.

SOCRATES: Well, some of these combinations are physical
c feelings restricted to the body; others belong exclusively to the

---

inscribed on the entrance to Delphi, the Greek religious centre. Much of Socratic and Platonic ethics is a philosophical justification of this and its brother, 'know yourself'.

soul; and there are still others we will come across which belong to the soul *and* the body. These combinations are pains
mixed with pleasures, but sometimes the sum of them is described as pleasant, sometimes as painful.

PROTARCHUS: Why?

SOCRATES: In the process of re-establishment or disruption, contrary feelings are felt simultaneously: for example, we
might be warming up when feeling cold, or cooling down
when feeling warm. We make an effort, I suppose, to gain the
one feeling and lose the other. When this happens we get a
bitter-sweet mixture, as it is called, which, when difficult to
relieve, causes an irritation which builds up into extreme *d*
excitement.

PROTARCHUS: That's very true.

SOCRATES: Don't some such combinations consist equally
of pain and pleasure, but some of one more than the other?

PROTARCHUS: Of course.

SOCRATES: You will grant, then, that some mixtures – *
the relief of pruritus that we mentioned just now, and of itches
in general – are the latter.[1] When pain predominates over
pleasure – when, say, the seething and the inflammation are
internal and not to be reached by rubbing and scratching which *
only dispel superficial irritation, then people sometimes apply
heat to the affected area, which removes the discomfort, and *e**
they might get immense pleasure from this. Alternatively,
they sometimes apply to the external area the opposite to the
internal disorder.[2] But whichever imbalance they choose,[3]
they get pain mixed in with their pleasure:[4] they are using *force*

1. Mixtures in which there is a predominance of one or the other: in the
particular case mentioned, of pleasure over pain (see 47a).

2. In this case, cold (allopathy) rather than heat (homeopathy).

3. Of heat or cold.

4. And presumably greater pain, since this is meant to be an example of
pain predominating over pleasure. This would, I suppose, have been clear to
Plato's contemporaries, to whom the sorts of remedies being outlined here
would have been familiar.

either to dispel what had been integrated, or to merge what had been dispersed,[1] so, as you will grant, they get pain along 47a with their pleasure.

PROTARCHUS: Perfectly true.

SOCRATES: On the other hand, when such mixtures are predominantly pleasant, then the person feels the painful element as an itching, a mild irritation, while he is stirred up by the far greater pleasant element, sometimes even to the extent of leaping about! His face goes all sorts of colours, his body adopts all sorts of postures, his breathing is just as variable; the pleasure drives him completely wild and makes him cry out in his frenzy!

b   PROTARCHUS: Too true.

SOCRATES: The result, my friend, is that thanks to these pleasures he is described, by himself and others, as 'almost dying with delight'; and the more uncontrolled and crazed he is, the more wholeheartedly he devotes himself to continuous pursuit of them. He calls them the greatest of pleasures, and he counts that man most fulfilled who spends his whole life with as many of them as possible.[2]

PROTARCHUS: Socrates, you have given a thorough description of all the factors which contribute to the opinion held by the majority of mankind.

c   SOCRATES: Thorough at least about the mixed pleasures which are found in sensations common to both the surface and the interior of the body, Protarchus. And we have already discussed those in which the soul contributes the opposite to the body, be it pain in immediate opposition to pleasure, or pleasure to pain;[3] the result is that both feelings combine to form a single mixture. We said that when someone has a lack he desires replenishment, and that pleasure comes from his anticipation,

---

1. The action of heat is to separate, of cold to merge (cf. 32a). Plato seems to be saying that either treatment may soothe the internal disorder, but, since these are extreme measures, at the expense of greater external pain.

2. cf. *Gorgias* 493e–494e.

3. See 36b.

pain from the lack. Although we didn't testify to this at the *d* time, what we are now saying is that in the innumerable cases where the soul is at odds with the body, the result is a single mixture of pain and pleasure.

PROTARCHUS: I don't think there's any doubt about that.

SOCRATES: Well, we've still got one last blend of pains and pleasures to discuss.[1]

PROTARCHUS: Which?

SOCRATES: The compound we said the soul by itself often gets.

PROTARCHUS: Yes, but what do we mean by that?

SOCRATES: Consider anger, fear, longing, grief, sexual *e* desire, jealousy, spite and so on: wouldn't you class these as pains which are peculiar to the soul?

PROTARCHUS: I would.

SOCRATES: It's provable that they are full of irresistible pleasures, isn't it? Or do we need to be reminded that, in moments of spleen and passion, 'it incites even the sage to wrath, and that it is sweeter by far than trickling honey',[2] and that grief and longing have pleasure mixed in with them along 48*a* with the pain?

PROTARCHUS: No, we don't. That's exactly what happens in these cases.

SOCRATES: And don't forget what happens to the audience at tragedies, will you? Even while they're weeping, they're enjoying themselves.

PROTARCHUS: Of course.

SOCRATES: Do you realize that at comedies too the soul's condition is one of mixed pleasure and pain?

PROTARCHUS: I don't quite understand.

---

1. See 46b–c.

2. Plato slightly misquotes (as elsewhere) a passage of Homer (here *Iliad* XVIII, 108–9). The original says: '(Anger) *which* incites even the sage to wrath, *which*, sweeter by far than trickling honey, (spreads like smoke in men's hearts).' Plato omits the subject, anger, presumably because the quotation was well enough known.

b   SOCRATES: That, Protarchus, is because it's not at all easy to see that this sort of experience *does* occur in this case.

PROTARCHUS: *I* don't find it easy, anyway.

SOCRATES: All the same, let's get to grips with it – more thoroughly, in fact, just because it is more obscure: then other cases of fusion of pain and pleasure will be easier to understand.

PROTARCHUS: Go on.

SOCRATES: All right. Take the word we mentioned just now, 'spite'. What do you think? Does it refer to a painful condition of the soul, or not?

PROTARCHUS: It does.

SOCRATES: Yet it's demonstrable that the spiteful man is *pleased* at his neighbours' misfortunes.

c   PROTARCHUS: Certainly.

SOCRATES: Now, an example of a harsh stroke of fate is the fatuous condition of ignorance![1]

PROTARCHUS: Of course.

SOCRATES: You can use this to understand the nature of what we find comical.

PROTARCHUS: Go on.

SOCRATES: There is a certain type of worthlessness which, to put it briefly, gets its name from a certain state of mind. Specifically, I mean that there is a worthless condition which is the opposite of the instruction in the Delphic inscription.

PROTARCHUS: Do you mean 'know yourself', Socrates?[2]

d   SOCRATES: I do. Clearly, the opposite of that would be if the inscription told us *not* to know ourselves at all.

PROTARCHUS: Of course.

SOCRATES: So, Protarchus, try to divide this into three.

PROTARCHUS: How? I'm not sure I can.

SOCRATES: You mean that *I*'ve now got to make the division?

1. Notice the assonance of 'fate' and 'fatuous': Plato is keen on such etymological puns.

2. cf. p. 111 n.1.

PROTARCHUS: Yes, and I'll even add 'please'.

SOCRATES: All right, then. Isn't it necessary for self-ignorance to be experienced in one of three ways?

PROTARCHUS: How?

SOCRATES: First, in respect of money: to believe oneself to *e* be richer than is warranted by one's estate.

PROTARCHUS: Yes, there are many who suffer from this.

SOCRATES: But there are even more who believe themselves to be taller, more good-looking and altogether better endowed physically than is in actual fact the case.

PROTARCHUS: Quite.

SOCRATES: But in my opinion by far the greatest number have fallen into the third kind of trap, which concerns what they have in their souls. They believe themselves to be more virtuous than they are.[1]

PROTARCHUS: Too true.

SOCRATES: Among the virtues, doesn't this especially 49*a* obtain where wisdom is concerned? People are always getting into arguments in which they utterly refuse to consider the other point of view; that is, they falsely believe themselves to be wise.[2]

PROTARCHUS: Of course.

SOCRATES: Now, it would be right to describe self-ignorance in any of its manifestations as a misfortune.

PROTARCHUS: Certainly.

SOCRATES: Well, we still need to differentiate between two forms of it, Protarchus, if we are going to see childish spite as a paradoxical mixture of pleasure and pain. 'What two forms?', you ask. All men fall into one of two groups, and *b* those who foolishly have this false estimate of themselves are no exception: so it is absolutely inevitable that some of them have strength and power, while others, you see, are the opposite.

PROTARCHUS: Yes, that follows.

1. This threefold division is clearly based on a division of goods into external, bodily and mental, which is common in Plato.

2. This mistake is the target of much scorn in Plato.

SOCRATES: Now, given this division, if you describe as comical those who are not only deluded but are also weak and unable to retaliate when mocked, you will be right. As for those who *are* able to retaliate, however, and are strong, if you call
c them frightening and dangerous, you couldn't describe them more accurately. You see, self-ignorance accompanied by strength is not just disgraceful, it's dangerous too: anyone who comes into contact with it, or anything like it, is threatened.[1] But the nature of ignorance in weak men made us classify it as comical.[2]

PROTARCHUS: You're quite right. But I still don't see the connection with a fusion of pleasure and pain.

SOCRATES: Well, you must first understand the nature of spite.

PROTARCHUS: Go on.

SOCRATES: Wouldn't you say that both pain and pleasure
d can be unjustified?

PROTARCHUS: Without a doubt.

SOCRATES: Isn't it the case that enjoyment of the misfortunes of others is neither unjustified nor spiteful if its object is someone who threatens you?[3]

PROTARCHUS: Of course.

SOCRATES: Sometimes, however, misfortune strikes a friend's affairs. Then it's pleasure, not pain, that is unjustified, isn't it?

PROTARCHUS: Of course.

SOCRATES: Didn't we say that ignorance is a misfortune *whoever* suffers from it?

PROTARCHUS: That's right.

SOCRATES: So what about when *friends* suffer from delu-

1. cf. *Laws* 863c–d.

2. cf. Aristotle, *Poetics* 1449a33–34.

3. cf. Sophocles, *Ajax* 79: 'Isn't laughing at enemies the most enjoyable laughter?' This is a standard tenet of Greek, pre-Christian, popular ethics: generally, do good to one's friends and harm to one's enemies. The historical Socrates, however, as opposed to the character in the later Platonic dialogues, seems to have rejected this tenet: see *Crito* 49.

118

sions of wisdom or beauty or any of the three kinds of delusion *e*
we distinguished just now? Are we to say that these delusions
are comical in the weak, abhorrent in the strong? Or are we to
deny this recent assertion of mine, and say instead that when
friends have this inability to harm anyone else, it is *not* comical?

PROTARCHUS: No, it is.

SOCRATES: And we agree that this condition, *qua* ignorance, is a misfortune, don't we?

PROTARCHUS: Certainly.

SOCRATES: When it amuses us, is it affording us pleasure
or pain?

PROTARCHUS: Pleasure, obviously. *50a*

SOCRATES: Didn't we say that what makes us feel pleasure
at friends' misfortunes is spite?

PROTARCHUS: It must be.

SOCRATES: Therefore the argument claims that when we
laugh at what is comical in friends – when, that is, we mix
pleasure with spite – then we are tempering our pleasure with
pain. For we agreed some time ago that spite is a painful condition of the soul; but we also agreed that amusement is pleasant, and on these occasions they both occur simultaneously.

PROTARCHUS: True.

SOCRATES: So now we can be sure that in grief, tragedy *b*
and comedy – not just when they are portrayed on stage, but
also in all the tragedy and comedy of life – pains and pleasures
are mixed. And the same goes for thousands of other cases.

PROTARCHUS: Even the most stubborn of opponents
couldn't fail to agree, Socrates.

SOCRATES: I hope not; but we proposed anger, longing,
grief, fear, sexual desire, jealousy, spite and so on as the things *c*
in which we would discover the now familiar subjects of this
discussion mixed together, didn't we?

PROTARCHUS: Yes.

SOCRATES: Well, our recent analysis was obviously restricted to grief, spite and anger, wasn't it?

PROTARCHUS: Of course.

SOCRATES: There are a lot left, then, aren't there?

PROTARCHUS: Yes.

SOCRATES: So why do you suppose that I concentrated on explaining the mixture in comedy? Wasn't it to convince you that it would be easy to explain the mixture that is found in *d* fear, sexual desire *et cetera*?[1] That when you had understood this you could release me from the necessity of prolonging the discussion by tackling the rest? *This* is what I want you to accept without reservations: that whether feelings are being felt by the body without the soul, or the soul without the body, or by both together, they are invariably mixtures of pleasure with pain. So tell me now, please: will you let me go, or will you keep me here till midnight? Perhaps you'll let me off if I just declare my willingness to complete the discussion with *e* you tomorrow. But for the time being I want to devote myself to the outstanding topics relevant to the decision which Philebus requires us to make.[2]

PROTARCHUS: Well pleaded, Socrates. Please continue with the outstanding issues, as you see fit.

SOCRATES: Well, naturally, after mixed pleasures, we are bound to turn to unmixed ones.

51*a* PROTARCHUS: Good.

SOCRATES: The next thing for me to do, then, is to try to show which they are. You see, I don't altogether believe those who claim that *all* pleasures are relief from pain. As I said, I regard such people as oracles, who reveal that some pleasures are merely thought to be pleasures, but aren't at all,[3] and that others – many others, in fact – give the impression of being great, but are kneaded together with pains and with cessation of the most agonizing discomfort of body and soul.[4]

b PROTARCHUS: Well, which pleasures would it be right to consider as true, Socrates?

1. See 48b.

2. Which of pleasure or reason is superior.

3. See 43d–44a.

4. Mixed pleasures, with a particular reference to 46d–e.

SOCRATES: Those which have to do with the colours we call beautiful, with figures, with most scents, with musical * sounds: in short, with anything which, since it involves imperceptible, painless lack, provides perceptible, pleasant replenishment which is uncontaminated by pain. *

PROTARCHUS: How do these objects achieve this, Socrates?

SOCRATES: You're right: the cases I'm talking about are not immediately obvious. I must try to make them so, how- c ever. By 'beauty of figures' I mean in this context not what most people would consider beautiful – not, that is, the figures of creatures in real life or in pictures. 'No', the argument says, [1] 'I mean a straight line, a curve and the plane and solid figures that lathes, rulers and squares can make from them.'[2] I hope you understand. I mean that, unlike other things, they are not *relatively* beautiful: their nature is to be beautiful in *any* situation, just as they are, and to have their own special pleasantness, which is utterly dissimilar to the pleasantness of d scratching. And I mean that there are colours which are analogously beautiful and pleasant. Do you see what I mean or not? *

PROTARCHUS: I'm trying to, Socrates. But you must make an effort too, to express yourself even more clearly.

SOCRATES: Well, by 'musical sounds' I mean unwavering, clear ones which produce a single pure phrase: they are not relatively beautiful, but are so in their own right, and they have innately attendant pleasures.

PROTARCHUS: Yes, that's so.

SOCRATES: Scents, on the other hand, produce a less di- e vine type of pleasure. Still, these pleasures don't necessarily

---

1. Here, as elsewhere in the dialogue (most strangely at 67b) and in other dialogues, Plato personifies the argument. It is not clear from the Greek where the words of the personified argument end and Socrates resumes *in propria persona*.

2. Notice the emphasis on the simplicity of the objects of pure pleasures. Simplicity was always Plato's aesthetic ideal since, in his view, the emotions which art arouses should be orderly: cf. *Republic* 398b ff. on music.

have pains mixed in with them:[1] so wherever or, rather, in whoever this happens, I find a case that entirely corresponds with the others. Nevertheless, if you follow me, there are two

* kinds of so-called pleasures here.[2]

PROTARCHUS: Yes, I follow you.

SOCRATES: Moreover, we mustn't exclude intellectual

52a pleasures, provided that they seem to us to contain neither hunger for information nor any initial pains as a result of hunger for information.

PROTARCHUS: Agreed.

SOCRATES: What about if someone has filled a gap in his knowledge, but later forgets it? Do you think there's any pain in this loss?

PROTARCHUS: Not inherently, perhaps. But suppose he needs the information and finds he's lost it: when he reflects on

b what's happened, he feels pain.

SOCRATES: Fair enough. But at the moment we're only concerned with what inherently happens to a man, not with his reflections.

PROTARCHUS: In that case you're right to say that lapse of memory is a painless element of intellectual pursuits.

SOCRATES: Well, there are two points to note about these intellectual pleasures: they are free from any mixture with pain, and they are the province of a few rare individuals, not the common run of men.

PROTARCHUS: Granted.

c SOCRATES: So now that we have made moderately clear the difference between pure pleasures and those which would be correctly described as almost entirely contaminated, we can explicitly attribute immoderation to intense pleasures, and its

1. cf. *Republic* 584b. The qualification is due to the fact that the pleasures of scent are more likely to be accompanied by a desire for food or whatever it is that is smelled. But the scent of, say, a rose garden has no such consequences. Cf. Aristotle, *Eudemian Ethics* 1231a 5 ff.

2. Two kinds: (i) some scents produce pure pleasures; (ii) others (see the previous note) produce mixed pleasures.

opposite, moderation, to those which are not intense: that is, we can attribute greatness and smallness respectively. And whether they occur commonly or rarely,[1] whether they penetrate body and soul to a greater or lesser extent,[2] we must say that they are members of our familiar indeterminate class, though some are moderate members.[3]

PROTARCHUS: You're quite right, Socrates.

SOCRATES: Next, here's an additional feature of theirs to consider.

PROTARCHUS: What?

SOCRATES: Which are we to say is related to truth: purity and uniformity, or intensity, frequency, size and contamination?

PROTARCHUS: What on earth are you getting at, Socrates?

SOCRATES: I want my cross-examination of pleasure and knowledge to be complete, Protarchus: when we find out if they both have some pure and some impure instances, we shall all be in a better position to make the required decision about them. We can do this when they both come forward for judgement in their pure form.

PROTARCHUS: Quite right.

SOCRATES: Well then, I suggest we choose for examination a *single* kind of thing we call pure, so as to make up our minds about *all* of them.[4]

PROTARCHUS: What shall we choose?

SOCRATES: With your approval, I suggest we make a particular study of whiteness.

PROTARCHUS: By all means.

1. It is assumed (see also 52b and d) that pure pleasures are rare.

2. See 33d: i.e. whether they are more or less intense.

3. Even moderate pleasures must be members of the indeterminate class (see 31a and *passim*), because even though in their case the preceding lack and movement is imperceptible, there is movement all the same.

4. This sort of reliance on induction is common in Plato, especially in the early Socratic dialogues.

SOCRATES: What *is* pure white, then? What are its parameters? Would we find it in the greatest quantity and extent of whiteness, or in the least tainted sample, which contains no other colour?

PROTARCHUS: Obviously in that which is contaminated as little as possible.

SOCRATES: Right. Isn't that the white we'll count as the
b truest and also the most beautiful of all whites, Protarchus, not the greatest extent or quantity?

PROTARCHUS: Yes, quite right.

SOCRATES: We're on perfectly safe ground, then, if we claim that a little pure white is whiter, finer and truer than a lot of mixed white.

PROTARCHUS: Quite right.

SOCRATES: Well, then, I don't think we need to continue with other examples of this phenomenon: this one entitles us to infer that a tiny little pleasure is, if uncontaminated by pain, always more pleasant, truer and finer than a large
c amount.[1]

PROTARCHUS: Assuredly so – further examples would add nothing.

SOCRATES: What about the following point? Haven't we been told that pleasure is always a 'process of generation' and has no 'existence' at all?[2] So here's another idea for us to consider, and we should be grateful to the subtle thinkers who are trying to tell us about it.

PROTARCHUS: Why?

---

1. sc. 'If that large amount is contaminated'. Plato omits this necessary qualification because he believes that, at least in the case of pleasure, large pleasures are *always* contaminated by pain: see 45a ff.

2. These vague terms (perhaps that is why Plato attributes them to 'subtle' thinkers) will be developed by Plato in what follows. It is not known who this philosopher was (for the singular, see 54d: the plural here presumably indicates his followers), but the antihedonist view he held fits in well with the assignment of pleasure to the indeterminate class: see the description of the indeterminate at 24a ff. Aristotle, *Nicomachean Ethics* VII.12, criticizes this section of the dialogue.

SOCRATES: If I may put some more questions to you, my dear Protarchus, all will be revealed.   *d*

PROTARCHUS: Carry on with your questions, then.

SOCRATES: Let's postulate two things: on the one hand that which exists in its own right, and on the other that which always aims at something else.

PROTARCHUS: What do you mean? What are they?

SOCRATES: The one is such that it is always very majestic; the other doesn't attain such heights.

PROTARCHUS: That doesn't explain much yet.

SOCRATES: I should think you too have noticed noble boys along with their manly admirers.[1]

PROTARCHUS: Certainly.

SOCRATES: Well, analogous to this particular pair, try to find a pair suitable for everything in general.   *e*

PROTARCHUS: Must I say it a third time? Please explain yourself more clearly, Socrates.

SOCRATES: It's not complicated, Protarchus. For all its banter, the argument is merely saying that things fall into two classes. On the one hand there are things which can only ever exist for some purpose; on the other hand there are those things which *are* the purposes for which the members of the first class come into existence at any time.

PROTARCHUS: All this repetition is helping me understand.

SOCRATES: Perhaps we'll soon understand it better, my young friend, as the argument progresses.   *54a*

PROTARCHUS: No doubt.

SOCRATES: There's another pair for us to consider.

PROTARCHUS: Consisting of what?

SOCRATES: On the one hand, the *generation* of anything; on the other hand, *existence*.

PROTARCHUS: I grant you this pair, 'existence' and 'generation'.

---

1. Who 'aims at' whom? Normal Greek practice (see *Symposium* 181c–184b) was for the older man to pursue the younger. In Athenian society, homosexuality was largely an upper-class phenomenon: hence 'noble'.

SOCRATES: Good. Now, which of them has the other as its purpose?[1] Are we to say that generation aims for existence, or existence for generation?

PROTARCHUS: Did I hear you ask whether what is called 'existence' exists entirely for the purpose of 'generation'?

SOCRATES: You heard aright.

b PROTARCHUS: Well really, Socrates! In effect your question comes to this: 'Tell me, Protarchus, would you say that ship-building *et cetera* occurs for the purpose of ships *et cetera*, or ships for the purpose of ship-building?'

SOCRATES: That's exactly what I mean, Protarchus.

PROTARCHUS: Why didn't you answer your own question, then, Socrates?

SOCRATES: I could have done, but you must take part in the discussion too.

PROTARCHUS: Very well.

c SOCRATES: Anyway, I maintain that paints, tools and materials in general are applied to anything so that generation can take place; that a particular process of generation occurs for the purpose of causing a particular thing to exist; and that generation always aims for existence.

PROTARCHUS: Very clearly put.

SOCRATES: Therefore, if pleasure is a process of generation, it is bound to occur in order that something might exist.

PROTARCHUS: Of course.

SOCRATES: Now, the end of any means partakes of goodness,[2] but the means, my friend, must be assigned to another class.

PROTARCHUS: Necessarily.

d SOCRATES: So if pleasure is a process of generation, we

1. Plato is assuming that the members of any pair, provided that it is a meaningful, non-artificial, pair, stand in this relation to one another. Hence, once the existence of such a pair has been agreed on, this question immediately follows.

2. What is good is by definition desirable; when we desire anything we devise means for getting it, but these means are not the end.

shall be right to assign it to a class other than that of the good.

PROTARCHUS: Quite right.

SOCRATES: So, as I said at the beginning of this discussion, we should be grateful to the person who indicated that pleasure has no existence whatsoever, but is a process of generation: obviously, you see, he's ridiculing hedonism.

PROTARCHUS: Indeed he is.

SOCRATES: And he would also mock those who treat such *e* processes as sufficient ends.

PROTARCHUS: What do you mean? What sort of people do this?

SOCRATES: All who, because of its pleasantness, enjoy the process of relieving their hunger or thirst or whatever it is that is relieved by some process, and so claim that they wouldn't want to live without thirst, hunger and all the related feelings one could mention.[1]

PROTARCHUS: Yes, that's what they claim, I suppose. *55a*

SOCRATES: Now, we would all agree that the opposite of the process of generation is the process of destruction.

PROTARCHUS: Necessarily.

SOCRATES: So whoever makes this choice is preferring destruction and generation to our familiar third life, the one in which we found no pleasure or pain, but only reason in the purest possible form.

PROTARCHUS: Hedonism is turning out to have some pretty absurd consequences, Socrates.

SOCRATES: Quite, especially considering the following point.[2]

PROTARCHUS: What?

---

1. If pleasure is remedial of pain, then in order to get pleasure, the hedonist must welcome pain, which is absurd: hedonism is self-contradictory. Democritus, a Presocratic philosopher of the late fifth century, makes a similar charge against hedonism (fragment 235). Callicles, the most extreme hedonist of the Platonic dialogues, seems prepared to accept this consequence at *Gorgias* 494b–c, 496c ff.

2. cf. *Gorgias* 497–9.

b SOCRATES: If anyone claims that goodness and beauty are properties of the soul, not of bodies or anything else, and, even where the soul is concerned, excludes courage, self-control, intellect and any other good attribute of the soul, and restricts goodness to pleasure – don't you think that's absurd?[1] As if that wasn't enough, the hedonist is also committed to the claim that someone who happens to be feeling pain rather than pleasure is, as long as the pain lasts, a bad man, even if he is in fact the most virtuous man in the world; and again, that someone feeling pleasure is, as long as the pleasure lasts, a better

c person in proportion to the intensity of his pleasure.[2]

PROTARCHUS: Nothing could be more absurd than all this, Socrates.

SOCRATES: Well now, we've tried to be thorough in our complete grilling of pleasure, but we mustn't leave it at that and show ourselves to be over-indulgent, so to speak, with intellect and knowledge. Propriety requires us to test the whole of this class for possible flaws; then, when we've discovered the purest kind, we'll be able to give our verdict, for which the truest kinds of both this class and of pleasure must come forward together.

PROTARCHUS: Right.

d SOCRATES: Isn't it the case that there are two kinds of scientific knowledge: the practical kind, and the kind used in teaching and education?

PROTARCHUS: Yes.

SOCRATES: The first point to consider concerns the technical sciences,[3] whether they can be divided into those which are closer to knowledge and those which are further away, and

1. This is an argument against the position that pleasure is the *sole* good, which Plato is attributing to Philebus. Here Socrates says that this places too much emphasis on pleasure: other things are valuable too.

2. An extreme hedonist might want to claim that any time we use the word 'good' properly, we should be able to substitute 'pleasant': see 60a.

3. The practical kind of scientific knowledge.

whether the first group should be thought to be purer, the *
second less pure.

PROTARCHUS: Yes, that's what we should consider.

SOCRATES: We must use the clearest examples, keeping
those of each group separate.

PROTARCHUS: What are they? How do we tell them
apart?

SOCRATES: Suppose arithmetic, measurement and weigh- *e*
ing were subtracted from all the sciences: the remainder of each
science would be pretty trivial.[1]

PROTARCHUS: It would indeed.

SOCRATES: In fact only speculation would be left, and the
training of the senses by experience and experiment. We
would have to use guesswork, which is commonly thought of
as science, if practice succeeds in making it dependable.   *56a*

PROTARCHUS: Yes, that's bound to be all that's left.

SOCRATES: Music-making seems to be full of this sort of *
thing, since it produces harmony by trained guesswork rather
than by measurement: for example, consider the playing of
stringed instruments, which uses guesswork to pinpoint the *
correct length of each string as it moves. Consequently, there
is little in it that is reliable, much that is uncertain.

PROTARCHUS: Very true.

SOCRATES: Moreover, it's demonstrable that the same *b*
goes for medicine, farming, helmsmanship and military command.

PROTARCHUS: Quite.

SOCRATES: On the other hand building, in my opinion,
since it usually employs measures and tools – things which im-
part considerable precision to it – is more of a *science* than most
branches of knowledge.

PROTARCHUS: How do you mean?

---

1. cf. *Republic* 522c: all sciences partake of number and calculation, to a
greater or lesser extent. *Republic* 509d–511e, 521c–534e is worth comparing
with this section of the *Philebus*.

SOCRATES: Look at ship-building, house-building and
c many other types of carpentry. As I see it, they use ruler,
lathe, callipers, chalk-line[1] and an ingenious try-square.[2]

PROTARCHUS: Quite, Socrates; you're right.

SOCRATES: We may distinguish, then, two groups of so-
called sciences: those which are related to music, in which less
precision is present, and those related to building, with more
precision.

PROTARCHUS: Granted.

SOCRATES: The most precise sciences, however, are those
we recently called essential.[3]

PROTARCHUS: I suppose you mean arithmetic and the
other sciences you mentioned along with it.

d SOCRATES: I do. Here again, however, Protarchus,
oughtn't we to speak of two sets of sciences, not one? What do
you think?

PROTARCHUS: Which sets do you have in mind?

SOCRATES: Take arithmetic first: shouldn't we distinguish between the common and the philosophical variety?

PROTARCHUS: What's the criterion for distinguishing
these two kinds of arithmetic?

SOCRATES: The boundary between them is clearly visible,
Protarchus. Some arithmeticians operate with unequal units:
for example, they add two armies together, or two cows, or
two things one of which might be the smallest and the other
the largest thing in the world.[4] Others, however, would never

1. A chalk-line is a piece of string ingrained with chalk and stretched taut
just above the wood or stone, so that when it is plucked, on the rebound it
marks the material with a straight line.

2. Plato's description of the try-square as 'ingenious' perhaps implies that
it was a recent invention. The only other use of the word in extant Greek
writings is in a second century B.C. Boeotian inscription (where, incidentally, it clearly means try-square, *pace* later ancient and medieval authorities, who
say the word (*epagōgion*) describes a tool used for straightening bent wood).

3. cf. 55e: they are essential because without them none of the sciences
have any precision at all.

4. cf. *Republic* 522c–e.

follow their example unless every unit, no matter how many *e* there are, is taken to be identical to every other unit. [1]

PROTARCHUS: You put that very well: since arithmeticians clearly fall into two classes, it makes sense for there to be two kinds of arithmetic.

SOCRATES: Now, what about calculation, which is used both commercially and philosophically, and measurement, which is used both in building and in philosophical geometry? What should we say? Are we to take each of them to be single *57a* or to consist of two kinds?

PROTARCHUS: I would follow the same route as before and vote for each of them being taken to consist of two kinds.

SOCRATES: You'd be right; but do you realize why we've brought all this out into the open?

PROTARCHUS: I think so, but I'd like to hear your explanation of the matter.

SOCRATES: In my opinion this discussion of ours has the same purpose now as when we embarked on it: it's looking for a counterpart to the pleasures we examined; [2] the stage the inquiry has now reached is the posing of the following question: do branches of knowledge, like pleasures, differ from one *b* another in purity?

PROTARCHUS: Yes, that's clearly the purpose of our exercise.

SOCRATES: Let's look back on the discussion, then: didn't

1. See *Republic* 510b–e on this mathematical assumption.

2. This is fair enough: we know that eventually we are to form a life out of some pleasures and some sciences. Nevertheless it is unsatisfactory in that no explicit grading of pleasures was given as it is now being given for sciences. We know (53b) that unmixed pleasures are 'truer' than mixed ones, but we have not been told that some mixed pleasures are truer and purer than others, as are some branches of knowledge. But given that unmixed pleasures are purest because they lack (perceptible) preceding pain, Plato may have in mind an implicit grading of mixed pleasures according to how much pain precedes them. Thus the mixed pleasures of a healthy person would be purer and truer than those of a sick person (see 45a ff.).

it first reveal differences between sciences with different domains in respect of relative certainty and uncertainty?

PROTARCHUS: Yes, it did.

SOCRATES: And among these sciences a certain one was mentioned as having a single name, which gave the impression of a single science. But now that the impression has been
c changed to that of *two* sciences,[1] the question of their certainty and purity arises, in the following terms: is the philosophical or the non-philosophical science more precise? Isn't that the upshot of our discussion?

PROTARCHUS: I think it raises the question very effectively.

SOCRATES: What are we to reply, then, Protarchus?

PROTARCHUS: Socrates, we're already faced with an incredibly huge difference between branches of knowledge in respect of certainty.

SOCRATES: That'll make it all the easier to reply, then, won't it?

PROTARCHUS: Of course. Here goes: not only is there a great deal of difference between the second kind of sciences and the others, but also, among the second kind, those undertaken
d by genuine philosophers are infinitely more precise and true in their use of measurements and numbers.

SOCRATES: We may take that statement of yours to be definitive and reliable. With that assurance, our response to cunning word-twisters[2] is . . .

PROTARCHUS: What?

SOCRATES: . . . that there are *two* techniques of arithmetic, *two* techniques of measurement, and so on for many other related sciences, which have this duality despite having been allotted a common name.

1. The single science of arithmetic has been divided into philosophical and common arithmetic.

2. e.g. Protagoras of Abdera, the eminent 'sophist' of the fifth century, who denied the validity of pure geometry on the grounds that there was no empirical evidence for, say, a line touching a circle at only a point. To this sort of thesis Plato's distinction is the proper reply. Protagoras' rhetorical teaching also gained him the reputation of being a cunning word-twister.

PROTARCHUS: We'd better wish *bon voyage* to this answer e
of ours, Socrates, if they're as cunning as you say.

SOCRATES: These are the branches of knowledge we're
claiming to be the most precise, then, are they?

PROTARCHUS: Yes.

SOCRATES: But dialectic would spurn us, Protarchus,
were we to give precedence to any other science.

PROTARCHUS: What's *this* science now? How should we
describe it?

SOCRATES: Clearly, everyone would recognize the science 58a
in question to be the truest one. I mean, I imagine that anyone *
with the slightest degree of intelligence believes that by far
the truest knowledge is the one whose domain is that which
truly is what it is and is always constant. What about you? *
What would your verdict be on the matter?

PROTARCHUS: Well, Socrates, when I heard Gorgias
speak he often used to say that the art of persuasion is easily the
most outstanding science, the reason being that it enslaves
everything in voluntary, unconstrained submission to itself: it is, b
in other words, the most noble science by a long way.[1] I don't
know what to do now, though, if I'm to avoid taking sides
against either you or him.

SOCRATES: You were about to say 'taking up arms', I
think, but conscientiously objected to it!

PROTARCHUS: You can think what you want.

SOCRATES: It's not my fault if you've got the wrong idea,
is it?[2]

PROTARCHUS: What have I misunderstood?

SOCRATES: My dear Protarchus, I hadn't got around to
asking which science or which branch of knowledge is outstand- c

1. Gorgias was a famous sophist and orator of the fifth century. His views
on rhetoric are preserved in a speech 'In Praise of Helen', sections 8–14,
where, however, the power of words is said to be a sort of constraint. Rather
than speech being a benevolent noble, as Protarchus suggests, Gorgias there
says that it is a 'powerful despot'.

2. Protarchus thinks Socrates' and Gorgias' positions are mutually exclu-
sive; Socrates will say that they are not really opposed, since the provinces of
the sciences they each recommend are so different.

ingly powerful or noble or profitable. I was simply asking which one surveys that which is certain, precise and most true: this is what we're now looking for, even if it is easily overlooked since its practical benefits are slight. Now look, if you concede to Gorgias that his art is authoritative as regards utility in human affairs, you won't antagonize him; but as for the occupation I've been talking about — well, remember what I was saying earlier about whiteness: that even if slight in quantity, provided it is pure, it surpasses a large amount

d which is not pure, because it is the truest instance. The same goes now for branches of knowledge: when we've thought hard and taken into consideration everything we need to, we shouldn't consider which of them is profitable or prestigious, but which faculty of our souls is such as to love the truth and to go to any lengths for its sake. If there is such a faculty, we must examine it closely and make it the subject of our discussion, to see if we have good grounds for attributing purity of intellect and reason to it rather than to any other — to see, that is, if we need to look any further for the supreme science.[1]

e PROTARCHUS: Let me see, then: yes, I find it difficult to accept that any other branch of knowledge or any other science has closer contact with truth than this one.

SOCRATES: How did you reach this conclusion? Was it because it occurred to you that most sciences and their practi-

59a tioners rely on beliefs and enthusiastically inquire into matters of belief?[2] Do you realize that even if one of these people imagines he is inquiring into the real nature of things, he is in fact spending his life studying aspects of the world around us,

1. The contrast between rhetoric and philosophy is a recurrent theme in Plato's writings, most eloquently at *Theaetetus* 172c–177c.

2. This and the following sentences assume the dichotomy, found most clearly in the central books of the *Republic*, between knowledge, whose object is 'what is' or 'what is real (true)', and belief, whose object is the changing world of particular phenomena.

such as how it arose, or how it acts or is acted upon? Do you
think that's a fair statement or not?

PROTARCHUS: It is.

SOCRATES: So to undertake such a task is to work not
with things which exist eternally, but with things which were,
are and will be subject to generation, isn't it?

PROTARCHUS: Perfectly true.

SOCRATES: Now, speaking with all truth and precision,
could we attribute certainty to any of these things, when none *b*
of them has ever been, nor will be, nor is at the moment
constant?

PROTARCHUS: Of course not.

SOCRATES: It's impossible for things which have never
acquired any reliability at all to be the objects of anything
reliable, isn't it?

PROTARCHUS: Quite impossible, I should say.

SOCRATES: Therefore they aren't the objects of intellect or
any branch of knowledge which comprehends what is most
true.

PROTARCHUS: It seems not.

SOCRATES: So we must forget all about particular people –
you, me, Gorgias and Philebus – and just give evidence to
the following effect.

PROTARCHUS: What?   *c*

SOCRATES: That reliability, purity, truth and what we
call uniformity are properties either of things which are always
constant and invariant in being perfectly free from mixture, or
at least of their closest kin; and that everything else must be *
described as secondary and inferior.

PROTARCHUS: You're absolutely right.

SOCRATES: On the subject of descriptions for such things,
isn't the best course to reserve the finest names for the finest
things?

PROTARCHUS: I don't see why not.

SOCRATES: Aren't 'intellect' and 'reason' names which are
held in particular esteem?   *d*

PROTARCHUS: Yes.

SOCRATES: So these terms, properly used, are tailor-made for cases of thought about that which truly is what it is.

PROTARCHUS: Certainly.

SOCRATES: And they are exactly the terms which I put forward earlier as my candidates in the decision.[1]

PROTARCHUS: Of course they are, Socrates.

SOCRATES: So far, so good. Well, if we were likened to
e builders who have available the materials from which or with which to construct something, that would be an accurate simile for our position as regards the mixing of reason and pleasure with each other.[2]

PROTARCHUS: A very good simile.

SOCRATES: Next, then, shouldn't we undertake the mixing?

PROTARCHUS: Of course.

SOCRATES: Aren't there some points it would be better to refresh our memories about first?

PROTARCHUS: Which ones?

SOCRATES: We've reminded ourselves of them before, but
60a I think there's value in the saying that a good point should be repeated two or three times in an argument.

PROTARCHUS: Of course there is.

SOCRATES: God speed us, then. I think the earlier resumés went something like this.[3]

PROTARCHUS: What?

SOCRATES: Philebus claims that pleasure is the proper

1. Actually, Socrates had earlier included even belief (when true) among his candidates, which has now been firmly distinguished from 'intellect and reason'. Notice how the partisans of pleasure are assumed to be advocating base pleasures, while Socrates now claims to be advocating only the highest branches of knowledge.

2. The simile is continued in 61a–b, 63b–e and 64c with the idea of the home of the good and the cohabitation of reason and pleasure in it.

3. cf. 11b–c, 19c–d.

goal for all beings, that everyone should aim for it,[1] that it is the good for everyone, and that the two terms 'good' and 'pleasant' should both be applied to a single phenomenon with a single nature.[2] Socrates, however, maintains that just as *b* there are two terms, so there are two things here, not one: the good is not the same as the pleasant; and he claims that more goodness attaches to reason than to pleasure.[3] Isn't that what we said before, Protarchus?

PROTARCHUS: Certainly.

SOCRATES: Can we still agree, as we did before, on a further point?

PROTARCHUS: What?

SOCRATES: That the good differs from other things in the following respect.

PROTARCHUS: How?   *c*

SOCRATES: Any creature that ever possessed it utterly and completely, with no possibility of ever failing to have it, would never lack anything else, since it would be in possession of what is absolutely perfect and sufficient.[4] Isn't that so?

PROTARCHUS: Yes, it is.

---

1. Psychological hedonism is the thesis that all creatures do, inevitably, pursue pleasure; ethical hedonism that they should do so, whether in fact they do or not. Here, then, Socrates is attributing ethical hedonism to Philebus. There has been no explicit assertion of this earlier in the dialogue. Probably Plato was not aware of the distinction, and we should see Philebus' view as 'all creatures do as they ought in pursuing pleasure'.

2. cf. *Protagoras* 355b ff. on the interchangeability of 'good' and 'pleasant'. This implies (see also 55b) that pleasure is the *sole* good: there are no other goods. This is in harmony with the formulation of Philebus' position at 11b, that pleasure is *the* good (see also 20e ff.), but not with 19c, where the formulation that pleasure is the *highest* good could be taken to allow other lesser goods; but this would place too much emphasis on the verbal formulation of 19c.

3. See 11b, 19d where Socrates' claim is not that reason is *the* good, only that it is better than pleasure.

4. See 20d.

SOCRATES: Didn't we set up a theoretical experiment in which we assumed a life consisting in turn of each ingredient in isolation from the other, so that pleasure was unmixed with reason, and reason similarly had not the slightest trace of pleasure?[1]

PROTARCHUS: We did.

SOCRATES: We weren't convinced that either of them was
d sufficient for any creature, were we?

PROTARCHUS: Of course not.

SOCRATES: If we made any mistake then, now's the time for someone to bring the issue up again and correct us. He should assume memory, reason, knowledge and true belief to be conceptually the same, and see if without them he would be happy to have or get anything – anything at all, that is, let alone pleasure, however extensive or intense it may be, when he could not truly believe that he is feeling pleasure, nor could he recognize any feeling at all, nor again could he retain even
e for an instant any memory of the feeling. As regards reason too, he should say whether the possession of reason completely divorced from pleasure, even the briefest pleasure, is preferable to the possession of reason together with some pleasures, as well as seeing whether the possession of all pleasures with no reason is preferable to the possession of all pleasures with some reason.

PROTARCHUS: Of course it isn't, Socrates; there's no need to repeat these questions.

61a SOCRATES: So neither of them is what is perfect, universally desirable and absolutely good, is it?

PROTARCHUS: Certainly not.

SOCRATES: Well, we've got to find out what the good is, preferably in detail, but even a rough idea will do, otherwise we won't know which candidate to award the second prize to, as we put it.

PROTARCHUS: You're quite right.

SOCRATES: Haven't we found a route towards the good?

1. See 20e ff.

PROTARCHUS: What?

SOCRATES: It's just like trying to find someone: in your search it would be a great help, I imagine, to be told exactly *b* where he lives.

PROTARCHUS: Naturally.

SOCRATES: Well, now it's the good that we're looking for, and the argument has reaffirmed its original suggestion that we look for it in the mixed, not the unmixed, life.

PROTARCHUS: Quite.

SOCRATES: Still, the chances of a clearer view of our quarry will be increased if we look in a fine compound rather than the opposite, won't they?

PROTARCHUS: Considerably increased.

SOCRATES: So we must pray to the gods, Protarchus, as we now begin to form a mixture – to Dionysus or Hephaestus or *c* whichever god presides over blending.[1]

PROTARCHUS: Quite.

SOCRATES: In fact it's just as if we were wine-servers with, on the one hand, supplies of pleasure, which in our simile would be honey, and also of reason, which would be a sobering, non-alcoholic supply of plain, wholesome water; from these we must devote ourselves to producing the finest of mixtures.[2]

PROTARCHUS: Of course.

SOCRATES: So here's your first question: if we were to mix *d* pleasure in its entirety with reason in its entirety, would this maximize our chances of attaining the correct mixture?

PROTARCHUS: Possibly, but . . .

1. This blanket invocation of a plurality of gods is a rarer form in ancient prayers than the one which makes sure of the correct title of a *single* deity (see p. 53 n.2). Dionysus would be invoked in his function as wine-blender; Hephaestus as maker of metal alloys (or perhaps as wine-server to the gods).

2. The terms of the simile are not quite clear: the beginning of the sentence suggests the ancient practice of mixing honey and water into wine, which it was the wine-waiter's job to do; but the end suggests a wine of only honey and water, i.e. mead. The latter image is more appropriate since there is no third ingredient, analogous to wine, in the good life.

PLATO

SOCRATES: But it's risky: I think I can suggest a safer way to mix them.

PROTARCHUS: Go on.

SOCRATES: We found that, in our opinion, some pleasures are more true than others, and also that some sciences are more precise than others, didn't we?

PROTARCHUS: To be sure.

SOCRATES: In fact we found that the difference between
e sciences is that one focuses on things that are subject to generation and destruction, the other on things which aren't subject to these processes but which exist for ever in a constant and unchanging condition. When we examined this latter science in respect of truth, we concluded that it was more true than the former.[1]

PROTARCHUS: That's right, we did.

SOCRATES: What about considering the result of mixing the truest portions of each together, then? Would this mixture be sufficient to provide us with the most attractive life as its end-product, or do we need something else besides these ingredients?

62a PROTARCHUS: No, I think this is the right move.

SOCRATES: So imagine a man whose reason comprehends the true nature of justice,[2] whose understanding keeps pace with his intellect, and who also has a similar grasp of every other reality.

PROTARCHUS: All right.

SOCRATES: Can we say he is *sufficiently* endowed with knowledge, when he has the measure of the ideal circle and the ideal sphere, which belong to the divine realm, but knows nothing about this sphere we inhabit or about the circles that
b are found here, not even when it comes to using measures and circles in building and so on?

1. See 58a ff.

2. In Platonic terms 'the true nature of justice' is something which 'exists for ever in a constant and unchanging condition'.

PROTARCHUS: The idea of being restricted to the divine sciences, Socrates, is ridiculous.

SOCRATES: What? Do you mean that, for all its unreliability and impurity, we should toss into our mixing-bowl the science which uses imperfect rulers and circles as well?

PROTARCHUS: We have to, if any of us is even to find his way home when he wants to.

SOCRATES: Music-making too, when we said a short *c* while ago that it is full of guesswork and bluff and consequently lacks purity?

PROTARCHUS: I think we have to, at least if our life is ever to be any kind of life at all.

SOCRATES: It follows that you want me, like a doorman buffeted and pressed by a crowd, to give way – to throw the doors open and let *all* the branches of knowledge pour in together, the pure mingling with the less pure. Isn't that right?

PROTARCHUS: I don't see what harm all the others can *d* do, Socrates, given possession of the first ones.

SOCRATES: So am I to allow all of them to pour into our pool – a regular 'watersmeet', as Homer rather poetically puts it?[1]

PROTARCHUS: Certainly.

SOCRATES: Done. But we must get back to our supply of pleasures: our intention of blending the ingredients by starting * with the true portions of each was foiled by our finding all forms of knowledge equally attractive, so that we let them jump the queue and enter *en masse* before pleasures. *e*

PROTARCHUS: That's very true.

SOCRATES: It's time for us to confer about pleasures as well, then, to see if we should also let all of them in *en masse*, or if in this case we should give precedence to true ones.

PROTARCHUS: It's far less risky to pass the true ones first.

1. *Iliad* IV, 452–4 (E. V. Rieu's translation): '. . . two mountain rivers . . . mingle their torrents at a watersmeet'.

SOCRATES: In they go, then. What's the next step? If some pleasures are necessary, as were some branches of knowledge, shouldn't they be mixed in too?[1]

PROTARCHUS: Of course — well, I suppose so, provided they *are* necessary.

63a SOCRATES: It might even be the same as it was with the sciences, where we found that it is not just harmless but actually beneficial to command them *all*, throughout one's life. So if that's in effect what we're saying about pleasures too — if it is advantageous and harmless for us all to spend our lives enjoying every kind of pleasure, then they must *all* be included in our mixture.

PROTARCHUS: What are we to say about them, then? What are we to do?

SOCRATES: You shouldn't look to us for an answer, Protarchus, but to pleasure and reason themselves: you should ask them about each other, along the following lines.

b PROTARCHUS: What?

SOCRATES: 'O Benevolent Ones, I address you by the name of pleasures, or by whatever name you wish to be known;[2] tell me, wouldn't you prefer to cohabit with reason in its entirety rather than live apart from reason?' I imagine there's only one answer they could give to that.

PROTARCHUS: What?

SOCRATES: We've already said as much: 'It's not possible, on the whole,[3] nor is it profitable, for any group to exist in
c solitary, unadulterated isolation. No; we think that knowledge, which is the best of the groups, should cohabit with us, so that knowledge of everything else is included, but especially

---

1. 'Necessary': sc. to make the good life practicable.

2. cf. p. 53 n.2. Are all pleasures being addressed, in which case this is sheer parody, or only the pure ones, in which case their deification is semi-serious? Given the Platonic nature of their reply, the latter is probably correct. Therefore Plato's hesitation about calling them 'pleasures' is due to the lingering negative connotations of the term.

3. This qualification is presumably included to allow for the idea that the gods can live a life of reason alone, as animals can live a life of pleasure alone.

so that each of us can have self-knowledge[1] to the greatest   *
possible extent.'

PROTARCHUS: 'Well said there' will be our comment.

SOCRATES: Right. Now, next it is the turn of reason and
intellect to be questioned: 'Do you need any pleasures in the
mixture?' we would inquire of intellect and reason. 'It depends
what you mean by pleasures,' would probably be their reply.

PROTARCHUS: It probably would!

SOCRATES: To which we have a rejoinder: 'We know   d
about *true* pleasures,' we'll say, 'but do you also need to share
your house with pleasures which are very great and intense?'
'Of course not, Socrates,' they would probably say. 'There's no
end to the trouble they make for us: with their frenzied irrationality they disturb the souls we inhabit;[2] they prevent the   *
conception of our kind and, if a child of ours *is* born, they in-   e
variably spoil him utterly by making him lazy and hence
forgetful. No, the pleasures you could count as members of our
household are the ones you called true and pure. In addition to
these[3] you should include in the mixture the pleasures which a
healthy, self-controlled man has, and in general all those pleasures which accompany every kind of virtue, as if they were
attendants on some deity.[4] It would be highly illogical for
anyone who wanted to discover the finest possible blend and
mixture, and the least turbulent one, to combine with intellect the pleasures which accompany self-indulgence and other
forms of vice. After all, what he's trying to learn from this   64a
mixture is what the good is, for man and in the universe, that
is, how, conceptually, he should picture the mixture.' Won't
we say that intellect has replied on behalf of himself, memory

1. So that the nightmarish situation of 21a–e and 60d is avoided.

2. The idea that pleasure hinders thought is expressed by Plato elsewhere
(e.g. *Phaedo* 64d–67d), as well as by other Greek thinkers.

3. This is a concession to provide a life which, while still good, is more
likely to be realized than one which contains only pure pleasures.

4. The mention of health confirms the suggestion made on p. 131 n.2:
these necessary pleasures are mixed, but minimally so, and thus are suitable
for a life which is to be both good and not over-austere or unrealizable.

and true belief in a reasonable and – not surprisingly! – intelligent way?[1]

PROTARCHUS: Absolutely.

SOCRATES: There's something else that's necessary too, in that without it nothing would ever take place.

b PROTARCHUS: What?

SOCRATES: Whatever lacks *truth* in its blending could never truly be generated so as to remain in existence once generated.

PROTARCHUS: Of course it couldn't.

SOCRATES: Exactly. Now, if this mixture is incomplete in any way, it's up to you and Philebus to point it out, because *I* think that this thesis leaves nothing to be desired as a sort of immaterial system for the management of animate matter.

PROTARCHUS: Well, Socrates, you can count on me to second that.

c SOCRATES: We wouldn't be too wrong, then, if we said that we are now standing on the threshold of the dwelling-place of the good, would we?

PROTARCHUS: *I* don't think so.

SOCRATES: Therefore we must decide what we take to be the most important element in the mixture: what is it that is most responsible for making this life attractive to everyone[2]? That is the next question because, once it's settled, we'll be in a position to consider whether this element is so constituted as to have, in the universal scheme of things, more kinship and affinity with pleasure or with reason.[3]

d PROTARCHUS: Right. That has the greatest bearing on our verdict.

SOCRATES: But look, any mixture can be at one or the

---

1. There is a pun in the Greek which is impossible to capture in translation without gross awkwardness: Plato talks of intellect 'having itself' – 'having intellect' being a Greek phrase for 'intelligently' (Euripides makes the same pun at *Iphigeneia in Aulis* 1139). For the pun on 'reasonable' see also 23a.

2. As it must be if it is the good life: see 20d.

3. See 22d.

other end of the value-scale, and where mixtures in general are concerned, it's not difficult to see why.

PROTARCHUS: What do you mean?

SOCRATES: Something which I suppose all men are aware of.

PROTARCHUS: What?

SOCRATES: That any kind of mixture which fails to be moderate and proportionate is bound to do away with its components and, above all, itself. One can't honestly say that there's a mixture in this sort of case, but rather an unmixed *e* confusion that really brings confusion on those who have it![1]

PROTARCHUS: Perfectly true.

SOCRATES: In every case, however, moderation and proportion seem, in effect, to be beauty and excellence.[2] So now this property we're looking for, goodness, has taken refuge in beauty.

PROTARCHUS: Quite.

SOCRATES: And we've already said that truth has been included in the mixture, along with these properties.

PROTARCHUS: Yes.

SOCRATES: Therefore if we are unable to net the good in a *65a* single concept, we must use three to capture it, namely beauty, proportion and truth. This is our position: supposing these three to be a single unit, we could not go wrong if we held it responsible for the components of the mixture, in the sense that, *qua* good, it makes the mixture good too.

---

1. This last somewhat extravagant claim seems to be made only for the sake of the etymological pun contained in it: the Greek word for 'trouble' (*sumphora*) originally means 'conjunction (of events)' — so, literally, 'an unmixed conjunction (of ingredients), a real conjunction (of events) for those who have it'. However the point of the paragraph is clear enough: one drop of wine in a glass of water is disproportionate; the mixture 'does away with its components' in that the wine can no longer be said to exist, 'and with itself' in that it cannot be said to be a real mixture.

2. Or 'virtue' (*arete*): all the words here used could have a specifically human application, particularly relevant to the ethics of the dialogue, but Plato here subordinates that to a description of what obtains for mixtures in general.

PROTARCHUS: Absolutely right.

SOCRATES: Well, Protarchus, by now anyone should be in a position to decide whether pleasure or reason is more akin to *b* the greatest good and is more highly thought of by both men and gods.

PROTARCHUS: Clearly, but it's still better to argue it through.

SOCRATES: So let's apply each of the three criteria, one at a time, to pleasure and reason: we must see to which of the two we will assign *each* property on the grounds of closer kinship.

PROTARCHUS: You mean beauty, truth and moderation?

SOCRATES: Yes. All right, Protarchus, first consider *c* truth. In doing so, concentrate on three things – intellect, truth and pleasure – and, without hurrying, satisfy yourself about whether pleasure or intellect is more closely related to truth.

PROTARCHUS: Why delay? In my opinion, you see, there's a world of difference between them: pleasure has no notion of honesty at all – in fact, there's a saying that where sexual pleasures are concerned, which are probably the most intense, even perjury is pardoned by the gods,[1] on the grounds that pleas- *d* ures, like children, are thoroughly irrational. Intellect, on the other hand, if not actually identical to truth, is at least the truest thing there is, by virtue of its incomparable similarity to truth.

SOCRATES: The next step, then, is to ask the same question about moderation: is it the property of pleasure rather than reason, or reason rather than pleasure?

PROTARCHUS: There's no difficulty in that question either: in my opinion, there's nothing that could conceivably be *less* moderate than pleasure and rapture, nor anything that could ever be *more* moderate than intellect and knowledge.

e SOCRATES: You put that well. But now your opinion on the third point, please. Does beauty attach more to intellect than to pleasure – which is to say, is intellect more beautiful than pleasure? Or is the opposite the case?

1. cf. *Symposium* 183b.

PROTARCHUS: Well really, Socrates! No one, asleep or awake, has ever seen or suspected the slightest trace of any incipient or existing or possible blemish in reason and intellect.

SOCRATES: Right.

PROTARCHUS: But, as you know, pleasures – and I think this is particularly true of the greatest pleasures – involve the person experiencing them in a ridiculous, if not utterly repulsive, display. This makes us self-conscious, and we keep these 66a pleasures as secret as possible, reserving all such activities for the hours of darkness, as if they should not be exposed to the light of day.[1]

SOCRATES: So your opinion, Protarchus, which you will announce to the present company and broadcast through messengers, is that as a possession, pleasure doesn't make the first or even the second grade, but that we should realize that goodness has somehow been caught above all in moderation and *
what is moderate, ordered and so on.

PROTARCHUS: Well, that's what the argument suggests.

SOCRATES: Then again, its second domain is proportion, b
beauty, perfection, sufficiency and everything of this kind.

PROTARCHUS: So it seems.

SOCRATES: Well, my intuition tells me you wouldn't be too far off the truth if you put intellect and reason in third place.

PROTARCHUS: You're probably right.

SOCRATES: What about the specifically psychic faculties we marshalled – branches of knowledge, sciences and beliefs which can be called correct? Aren't they ranked fourth after the *
first three, since they are more akin than pleasure to goodness? c

PROTARCHUS: Presumably.

SOCRATES: What about the pleasures we called pure, once we'd defined them as painless, some of which accompany these sciences which belong specifically to the soul, while others *
accompany perceptions?[2] Don't they gain fifth place?

PROTARCHUS: Probably.

SOCRATES: 'Let the system, the theme of your song, be no

1. cf. *Hippias Major* 299a.
2. See 51b ff.

more than six stages long,' as Orpheus says.[1] It looks as though in our discussion too the sixth decision is the final one.
d So there's nothing left for us to do now but take stock, as it were, of what's been said.

PROTARCHUS: Yes, we should do that.

SOCRATES: So, as our third libation 'to Zeus the Deliverer',[2] let's go through the argument, giving our evidence for the third time.

PROTARCHUS: What do you mean?

SOCRATES: Philebus proposed every form and variety of pleasure as the good.

PROTARCHUS: It seems that your recent expression, 'the third libation', meant a complete recapitulation of the argument, Socrates.

e SOCRATES: It did, and now I'll remind us of what came next. You see, I was aware of the points I've just expounded, so, since I found Philebus' thesis distasteful – well, it's not just his, it's what innumerable others usually think as well – I said that for *human* life intellect is far, far better than pleasure.

PROTARCHUS: You did.

SOCRATES: Yes, but I suspected that that was not the end of the matter, so I said that if anything turned out to be better than *both* of them, I would be a staunch ally of intellect against pleasure for the second prize, and that pleasure would forfeit even the second prize.

67a PROTARCHUS: Yes, that's what you said.

SOCRATES: And subsequently it *did* turn out, beyond the shadow of a doubt, that neither of them is sufficient.

1. Orpheus was a semi-legendary bard whom writers of religious and cosmogonical poetry over many centuries took as the founder of their 'school'. This is a fragment of one such cosmogonical poem. Probably the author meant by 'the system of your song' no more, by poetic periphrasis, than 'song', but Plato seems to intend us to remember his 'immaterial system for the management of animate matter' of 64b. Plato's sixth stage is presumably those necessary pleasures which it was agreed at 63e to include.

2. At banquets libations were poured in a certain order: first to Zeus and the Olympian gods; second to the heroes; and finally to Zeus the Deliverer. Hence the expression became proverbial for the final stage of anything.

PROTARCHUS: Perfectly true.

SOCRATES: Isn't it the case that by this argument both intellect and pleasure were each completely absolved from being the good itself, since they both lack independence, that is, sufficiency and perfection?

PROTARCHUS: Quite right.

SOCRATES: Once we'd found a third contestant which was superior to either of the others, however, it became clear that intellect is infinitely more closely related and akin than pleasure to the victorious concept.

PROTARCHUS: Of course.

SOCRATES: In fact the verdict the argument reached is that pleasure will take fifth place.

PROTARCHUS: So it seems.

SOCRATES: But not the first place – not even if all the *b* cows and horses, and the whole animal kingdom, claim it is, by their pursuit of pleasure. The popular assessment of pleasure as the mainspring of the good life is caused by relying on animals, as seers do on birds[1]: people imagine that beasts' predilections are more authoritative witnesses than those of arguments inspired by the Muse of philosophy.

PROTARCHUS: We all now agree, Socrates, that what you've said is perfectly true.

SOCRATES: Do you mean I can go now?

PROTARCHUS: There's still a little unfinished business, Socrates. I'm sure you won't give up before us, so I'll remind you of what's outstanding.

1. A common hedonistic argument runs: 'Pleasure must be the good, because all creatures aim for it.' cf. Philebus' taking account of animals at 11b and 60a.

BIBLIOGRAPHY

I append some suggestions for further reading, none of which assumes any knowledge of Greek.

The most recent translations of the *Philebus* are:

R. Hackforth, *Plato's Examination of Pleasure*, Cambridge, 1945 (reprinted as *Plato's Philebus*, Cambridge, 1972); translation with running commentary.

A. E. Taylor, *Plato: Philebus and Epinomis*, London, 1956; translation with lengthy introduction.

J. C. B. Gosling, *Plato: Philebus*, Oxford, 1975; translation with difficult, but rewarding, philosophical commentary.

Those who want to pursue Platonic studies further could start with I. M. Crombie, *An Examination of Plato's Doctrines*, 2 vols., London, 1962–3.

Two useful modern studies of pleasure and related issues are A. Kenny, *Action, Emotion and Will*, London, 1963; and J. C. B. Gosling, *Pleasure and Desire*, Oxford, 1969.

TEXTUAL APPENDIX

The text of the *Philebus* is difficult and has therefore suffered
from considerable corruption. I have translated the text of
J. Burnet (Oxford, 1901) except at the following points,
marked in the translation by an asterisk. I here merely give
the text I have adopted and the original source of the
reading or conjecture: justification of the readings would
be out of place here.

12d8–e1 Kamerbeek: πῶς γάρ; ἡδονή γε ἡδονῆι μὴ οὐχ
ὁμοιότατον

14b1 MSS: τοῦ ἀγαθοῦ

14b3 Grovius: ἐλεγχομένω

15b4–8 Badham: μίαν ταύτην, μετὰ δὲ τοῦτ᾽ . . .
γίγνεσθαι;

19a1 Paley: τίνα

21d1 TW: ἄλλως πως

22c7 Waterfield: ἀμφισβητήσω ὑπὲρ νοῦ

23d2 Apelt: τις καὶ ἄνους

24b4 T: καὶ τῶι ψυχροτέρωι

26d4 Apelt: ὅτε . . . οὐκ

27d8 Schütz: μικτὸν ἐκεῖνο

27e8, 28a1 Bekker: πανάγαθον, πάγκακον

28a3–4 Waterfield: τούτω δὴ σοι . . . γεγονότε ἔστων

29a11 Jowett: οἱ χειμασόμενοί φασιν

29c5 MSS: ἄρχεται

30e1–2 Bekker, Stallbaum: [τῆς] τοῦ πάντων αἰτίου
λεχθέντος· τῶν τεττάρων δ᾽ἦν ἡμῖν ἓν τοῦτο

31a1 Bekker: νοῦς δήπου

TEXTUAL APPENDIX

63d6 Waterfield: διὰ μανικῆς ἀνοίας

66a7–8 T. Waterfield: καὶ πάντα ὁπόσα τοιαῦτα, χρὴ
νομίζειν τὴν ἀγαθοῦ ἡιρῆσθαι φύσιν.

66b8 Waterfield: οὐ τέτακται

66c5 Waterfield: ἐπονομάσαντες, τῆς ψυχῆς αὐτῆς
ἐπιστημαῖς,

32a9 Stallbaum: τοῦ ἀπείρου

33a8 MSS: τῶι . . . ἑλομένωι

34c1 Waterfield: ἀναμνησθῆναι μνήμας

36b6 MSS: τοῖς χρόνοις

39a4 MSS: τοῦτο τὸ πάθημα

40e6 Apelt: κἀχρήστους

44b7 T: οὐ μανθάνεις.

45b9 Hackforth: ἀποπληρούμενοι

46a11 Waterfield: ἤ λύπην, σύμμεικτον⟨ὄν⟩;

46a12 T: τοῦτό γε

46d7–9 Waterfield: λέγε δὴ τὰς μέν, τὰς τῆς ψώρας
⟨ἰάσεις⟩ λεγομένας νυνδή, ταύτας εἶναι, καὶ τὰς τῶν
γαργαλισμῶν. ὅταν πλείους λῦπαι τῶν ἡδονῶν γίγνονται
– ὁπόταν . . .

46d9 MSS: ὁπόταν ἐντὸς

46e2 MSS: ἀπορίαις

47e6–9 Waterfield: ἤ δεόμεθα ὑπομιμνῄσκεσθαι τὸ "ὥς
τ᾽ ἐφέηκεν" τοῖς θυμοῖς καὶ ταῖς ὀργαῖς τὸ "πολύφρονά
περ χαλεπῆναι, ὥς τ᾽ πολὺ γλυκίων . . .

51b4 Waterfield: ἠχὰς τῶν φθογγῶν

51b6–7 MSS: καθαρὰς λυπῶν

51d2 Waterfield: καλὰ καὶ ἡδέα εἶναι

51e5 MSS: δύο λεγομένων

52c4–5 Waterfield: καὶ τὸ μέγα καὶ τὸ σμικρὸν αὖ· καὶ . . .

52c6 Stallbaum: [τῆς] τοῦ

52c7 Waterfield: φερομένας

52d1 B: τὰς δὲ τῶν

52d8 Waterfield: μίαρον

55d7 Badham: καθαρώτερα

56a3 Badham: μουσικὴ τοιούτων

56a5 Hermann: αὐτῆς ψαλτικὴ

58a1 Waterfield: δῆλον ὅτι ἅπας ἂν τήν γε νῦν λεγομένην
⟨ἀληθεστάτην⟩ γνοίη·

58a2 Badham: τὸ ὄν [καὶ τὸ] ὄντως

59c4 Diès: ἤ περὶ ὅσ᾽

62d8 Apelt: αὐτὰ μειγνύναι

63c3 van Heusde: αὐτὴν αὑτὴν

MORE ABOUT PENGUINS
AND PELICANS

For further information about books available from Penguins please write to Dept EP, Penguin Books Ltd, Harmondsworth, Middlesex UB7 ODA.

In the U.S.A.: For a complete list of books available from Penguins in the United States write to Dept CS, Penguin Books, 625 Madison Avenue, New York, New York 10022.

In Canada: For a complete list of books available from Penguins in Canada write to Penguin Books Canada Ltd, 2801 John Street, Markham, Ontario L3R 1B4.

In Australia: For a complete list of books available from Penguins in Australia write to the Marketing Department, Penguin Books Australia Ltd, P.O. Box 257, Ringwood, Victoria 3134.

In New Zealand: For a complete list of books available from Penguins in New Zealand write to the Marketing Department, Penguin Books (N.Z.) Ltd, P.O. Box 4019, Auckland 10.

PLATO

THE REPUBLIC

Translated by Desmond Lee

Plato (427–347 B.C.), finally disillusioned by contemporary politics after the execution of Socrates, showed in his writings the enormous influence of that great philosopher. *The Republic*, his treatise on an ideal state, was the first of its kind in European thought. For Plato, political science was the science of the soul, and included moral science. *The Republic*'s emphasis on the right education for rulers, the prevalence of justice, and harmony between all classes of society, is as strong as its condemnation of democracy, which Plato considered encouraged bad leadership.

THE SYMPOSIUM

Translated by Walter Hamilton

Of all the Greek philosophers, Plato was perhaps the greatest. *The Symposium* – a masterpiece of dramatic dialogue – is set at a dinner party to which are invited several of the literary celebrities of Athenian society. After dinner it is proposed that each member of the company should make a speech in praise of love. A full discussion follows and the dialogue ends with a brilliant character sketch of Socrates by Alcibiades. Throughout Plato reveals, as few other authors have done, the beauty, power, and flexibility of Greek prose.

PLATO

THE LAST DAYS OF SOCRATES

Translated by Hugh Tredennick

The trial and condemnation of Socrates, on charges of heresy and corrupting the minds of the young, forms one of the most tragic episodes in the history of Athens in decline. In the four works which compose this volume – *Euthyphro, The Apology, Crito*, and *Phaedo* – Plato, his most devoted disciple, has preserved for us the essence of his teaching and the logical system of question and answer he perfected in order to define the nature of virtue and knowledge. The vindication of Socrates and the pathos of his death are admirably conveyed in Hugh Tredennick's modern translation.

GORGIAS

Translated by Walter Hamilton

To judge by its bitter tone Plato's *Gorgias* was written shortly after the death of Socrates. Though Gorgias was a Sicilian teacher of oratory, the dialogue is more concerned with ethics than with the art of public speaking. The ability, professed particularly by the Sophists, to make the worse cause appear the better, struck Plato as the source of all corruption. The dialogue's chief interest lies not in Gorgias' courteous outline of his art, but in the clash between Socrates, the true philosopher, and Callicles, a young Athenian of the stamp of Alcibiades, who brashly maintains that might is right.

PLATO

TIMAEUS AND CRITIAS

Translated by Desmond Lee

The *Timaeus*, in which Plato attempted a scientific explanation of the universe's origin, is the earliest Greek account of a divine creation: as such it has significantly influenced European thought, even down to the present day. Yet this dialogue and, even more, its unfinished sequel, the *Critias*, have latterly attracted equal attention as the sources of the Atlantis legend. Plato's exact descriptions of an antediluvian world have fermented the imaginations of hundreds of writers in this century and the last, and the translator has now appended an intriguing survey of Atlantis and of theories (crazy and plausible) about the vanished continent.

PROTAGORAS AND MENO

Translated by W. K. C. Guthrie

Plato held that philosophy must be a product of living contact between mind and mind, and his dialogues afforded him the means of reaching a wide audience. *Protagoras*, possibly his dramatic masterpiece, deals, like *Meno*, with the problem of teaching the art of successful living and good citizenship. While *Protagoras* keeps to the level of practical commonsense, *Meno* leads on into the heart of Plato's philosophy, the immortality of the soul and the doctrine that learning is knowledge acquired before birth.

PLATO

THE LAWS

Translated by T. J. Saunders

The reader of *The Republic*, Plato's best-known political work, may
well be astonished by *The Laws*. Instead of an ideal state ruled
directly by moral philosophers, this later work depicts a society
permeated by the rule of law. Immutable laws control most aspects
of public and private life, from civil and legal administration to
marriage, religion and sport. The rigours of life in Plato's utopian
Republic are not much tempered here, but *The Laws* is a much more
practical approach to Plato's ideal.

In his introduction Dr Saunders reinterprets the whole work and
also discusses the vexed question of Plato's totalitarianism.

PHAEDRUS AND LETTERS
VII AND VIII

Translated by Walter Hamilton

In the *Phaedrus* Plato (427–347 B.C.) is concerned with establishing
the principles of rhetoric. Through the mouths of Socrates and
Phaedrus he argues that rhetoric is only acceptable as an art when it
is firmly based on the truth inspired by love, the common experience of true philosophic activity. It is in this dialogue that Plato
employs the famous image of love as the driver of the chariot of
souls.

The seventh and eighth letters (which are accepted as genuine
amongst those attributed to Plato) provide fascinating glimpses into
the contemporary power struggle in Sicily and evidence his failure
to put into practice his theory of the philosopher-king.

Xenophon

THE PERSIAN EXPEDITION

*Translated by Rex Warner with an introduction
by George Cawkwell*

This account of the Ten Thousand, of their march into Persian to put Cyrus on the throne, of their total defeat at the battle of Cunaxa and of their heroic march back to the Black Sea remains one of the great adventure stories of history. Even if Xenophon (c. 430–354 B.C.), the Athenian general and historian whose sympathies lay with Sparta, sometimes rivals Julius Caesar for self-congratulation, it is impossible not to be drawn by his simple narrative of courage, skill and initiative and by the pride and piety of the band of Greeks cut off in a world of barbarians.

Apollonius of Rhodes

THE VOYAGE OF ARGO

Translated by E. V. Rieu

Written in the third century B.C., the *Argonautica* is the only full remaining account of Jason's voyage in quest of the Golden Fleece. Though Apollonius used the manner and matter of epic, he wrote from a personal viewpoint, as a critical observer. His understanding of human nature, his unerring eye for dramatic movement, and his quiet sense of humour give reality and spirit to this fantastic story of high romance and incredible adventure.

THE GREEK ANTHOLOGY

Edited by Peter Jay

The Greek Anthology is the famous collection of some 4000 poems assembled by Byzantine scholars nearly a thousand years ago. The poems, drawn from all over the Greek-speaking world, range from the seventh century B.C. through to the renaissance of Greek culture in Byzantium during the sixth century A.D.

This volume contains about 850 of these poems and is the largest selection ever to be published in verse translation. Arranged chronologically with a brief introduction to each poet, the poems cover every aspect of Greek life – epitaphs, satires, jokes, pastoral epigrams and poems of love and friendship. Over forty distinguished British and American poets have contributed to the translations.

'Will make them laugh, cry and think and I welcome it unreservedly' – Cyril Connolly in the *Sunday Times*.

'Such a collection has no possible foreseeable rival' – *The Times Literary Supplement*.

GREEK LITERATURE

Edited by Michael Grant

In this volume (previously published as *Greek Literature in Translation*), Michael Grant displays, as far as possible, the whole range of Greek poetry and prose, from Homer and Hesiod to the Hellenistic poets and the works of Ptolemy, Galen and Plotinus. His selection vividly demonstrates the extraordinary extent of Greek achievement in every literary field – in epics, lyrics and drama, in history, biography and oratory, in philosophy, criticism and satire, and in works of fundamental scientific thought.

Sophocles

THE THEBAN PLAYS

Translated by E. F. Watling

These three plays by Sophocles (496–406 B.C.), though they are all
based on the legend of the royal house of Thebes, were written at
different periods and dramatize different themes. *Antigone* is the
tragedy of a woman ruled by conscience, an over-confident king, and
a young man tormented by conflicting loyalties. *King Oedipus* is a
vast and living portrait of man without parallel in the Greek
theatre, and *Oedipus at Colonus* completes the story with the legend
of the passing of the aged hero.

Euripides

ALCESTIS AND OTHER PLAYS

Translated by Philip Vellacott

Euripides (484–407 B.C.) is seen in the three plays in this volume
as the sceptical questioner of his age. *Alcestis*, an early play in which
a queen agrees to die to save her husband's life, is cast in a tragic
vein, although it contains passages of satire and even comedy,
whilst *Iphigeneia in Tauris*, with its apparently happy ending,
melodramatically re-unites the ill-fated children of Agamemnon.
Hippolytus, however, is pure tragedy – the fatal impact of Phaedra's
unreasoning passion for her chaste stepson.